THE STO[RY OF]
THE GADSBYS

BY RUDYARD KIPLING

A H WHEELER & Co's

No 2

One Rupee

INDIAN RAILWAY LIBRARY

LAHORE.

The R. S. Surtees Society is most grateful to Lady Juliet Townsend (The Old Hall Bookshop, Market Place, Brackley) and to David Robertshaw (The Warminster Bookshop, 6 East Street, Warminster) for lending the books from which the covers and texts of the Kipling titles in the Indian Railway Library series have been – or are about to be – copied; we are also very grateful to John Saumarez Smith (G. Heywood Hill, 10 Curzon Street, London, W.1.) for most opportunely suggesting where we might find what we were looking for.

We were delighted when Philip Mason agreed to write Forewords for *Soldiers Three* and *The Story of the Gadsbys* and still more pleased when he agreed, with apparent alacrity, to provide Forewords for *In Black and White* and *Under the Deodars,* which we intend shall be avialable by April, 1987.

Our publication of *Soldiers Three* and *The Story of the Gadsbys* is by permission of Macmillan London Limited.

In our leaflet of May 1986 we advertised our books as facsimiles of the first editions published in the Indian Railway Library series in 1888, save for the addition, in the case of *Soldiers Three,* of four illustrations by A. S. Hartrick. After the issue of the leaflet we decided on the further additions to *Soldiers Three* of 'Danny Deever' and 'The 'Eathen'. It may be that some pre-publication subscribers subscribed on the assumption that we would do exactly what we said we would do and that to these we now owe such explanation as is available.

Professor Sir Angus Wilson has written that the exploits of the three soldiers are best read alongside *Barrack Room Ballads.*

An inattentive reader of 'In the Matter of a Private' might be left with the impression that the author made the fate of Private Simmons too light a matter. 'Danny Deever', No. 1 of *Barrack Room Ballads* and first published in the *Scots Observer* in February 1890 (which separates it by months, rather than years, from 'In the Matter of a Private', first published in April 1888), should correct any such impression.

Similarly some readers might just possibly suppose that 'With the Main Guard' was a callous indulgence of the public's taste for military vainglory, with a remarkable example of a late

Victorian's complacent idea of the devotion of the lower orders (at any rate, when in uniform) to the officer and gentlemanly class thrown in for good measure. Inclusion of 'The 'Eathen' may make it clear that 'With the Main Guard' is a story about comradeship – how Mulvaney, with some help from Ortheris, generously used his histrionic gift to rescue Learoyd from Giant Despair, to such effect that at the end of the story Learoyd is himself helping a comrade, or at any rate helping to help his child. In another story Learoyd and Ortheris perform a similar service for Mulvaney and, they having shifted Mulvaney away from tragedy to the ordinarily melancholy, the author unobstrusively moves all three on to cheerfulness by providing bottled beer – for free. Golly, how the Liberals must have hated him!

'The 'Eathen' first appeared in McClure's Magazine in 1896. Professor Sir Charles Carrington has said that the lines

'So, like a man in irons which isn't glad to go,
They moves 'em off by companies uncommon stiff an' slow.'

are the most compelling proof of Kipling's imaginative powers. He says that he would not have believed it possible for a man, who had never himself seen infantry move when required to close with the enemy, to pen such an exact description. So for those of us who have not been present on such occasions (Carrington has) the verses are informative.

We were over confident when we said in the leaflet that the covers were designed by Rudyard's father, Lockwood Kipling. All that is known with certainty (we now think) is that the covers were designed at the Mayo School of Art, Lahore, of which Lockwood was the Director.

We would have liked to have exercised our literary intuition by telling readers that the dog momentarily stationary behind Jock Learoyd's heels, on the cover of *Soldiers Three,* is a portrait of Rudyard's fox-terrier Vic (or Vixen as she is called when she appears in Literature). But a comtemporary of Rudyard, quoted by Angus Wilson, wrote that Vic was white "like a nice clean sucking pig" whereas the dog in the picture has extensive black markings. Rip, whom Mrs. DeSussa coveted, is a possibility.

Lastly, following our principle of telling the truth unless it is intolerably inconvenient, anyone who consults James McG.

Stewart's Bibliographical Catalogue of Kipling (published by Dalhousie University, Canada) will note some further divergences from the first Indian editions which we have not mentioned here.

James McG. Stewart is the chap. Borrowing a first Indian edition would be, at best, difficult and troublesome; and honest acquisition very expensive.

R.S.S.S.
Rockfield House,
Nunney, Nr. Frome,
Somerset. Aug. 1986

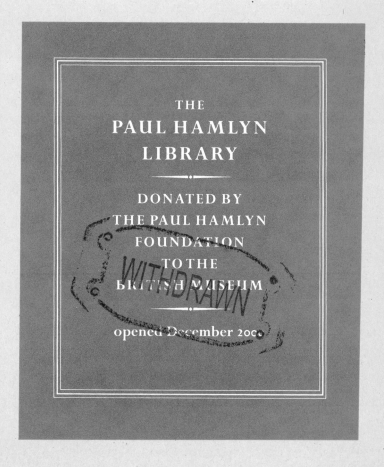

THE R. S. SURTEES SOCIETY

First published in this edition in 1986 by
The R. S. Surtees Society

Rockfield House
Nunney
Nr. Frome, Somerset

© This Edition and Compilation
The R. S. Surtees Society, 1986
ISBN 0 948560 04 5

Produced in Great Britain
by MARCH PRESS
Adderwell Road, Frome, Somerset.

FOREWORD

In Charles Carrington's careful, reliable biography of Rudyard Kipling, *The Story of the Gadsbys* is referred to as 'a short, sentimental novel, told in dialogue'. Angus Wilson, in his more recent life, calls it 'a bitter marriage comedy' and speaks of Gadsby's 'death by marriage.' Both are right; it is at the same time sentimental and cynical. It was one of the six collections published in 1888 by Wheeler's Indian Railway Library, paperbacked, at One Rupee each, and is here republished in as near as possible the original form.

Is it really: *A Tale without a Plot,* as the sub-title calls it? How much is irony and satire? The scene opens in Minnie's bedroom in Simla, where she is exchanging girlish confidences with her best friend; they include the famous saying that to be kissed by a man who doesn't wax his moustache is like eating an egg without salt. Captain Gasdsby is coming to take Minnie's mamma riding but she is not dressed and Minnie, who doesn't like him, has to entertain him for a few minutes. She eyes his moustache, beautifully waxed, finds she does after all like him better than she thought – and begs him not to keep her mother out late because of her rheumatism. Three weeks later they are engaged.

The scene shifts to the Club in the station in the plains from which Gadsby is on leave and the news arrives that he has been 'caught'. There are jocular clichés and then speculation about Mrs. Herriott, to whom he seemed to have been devotedly attached during the last cold weather. At the club, they do not seem to have heard that, in the repulsive slang of the day, he has been 'mashing' Minnie's mamma since he last saw Mrs. Herriott. Gadsby is next seen in another hill station, where he has gone to break it off with Mrs. Herriott; this he does clumsily and brutally, stamping on her love to kill it finally, not liking the unpleasant job but showing no sign of concern for her feelings. Then, on the morning of the wedding, we see his best friend 'getting his man to the starting-post', with more heavily-used witticisms of the order of 'the condemned man ate a hearty breakfast'. We listen to honeymoon prattlings at one of the rest houses on the Hindustan-Tibet road – and there can be no doubt that these are sentimental – and a few months later, we arrive at the central point of the story. Gadsby's serious professional interest is a scheme for reducing the weight to be carried by a troop-horse in war; he is deeply immersed in balancing weight against strength when Minnie interrupts; she wants sympathy and comfort, a kiss and the opportunity to whisper shyly her little secret.

The bride in India was usually separated from her mother-in-law by six thousand miles. She had nothing to contend with but bachelor habits, tiresome old friends, old loves, sometimes a devoted old bearer – and work. There have been critics of Kipling who thought he preached a gospel of work – and so he did, though work was not his only god. But the frivolous young woman who won't take a man's work seriously is a recurrent theme, beginning with *Wressley of the Foreign Office* in Plain Tales. Minnie wanted to 'share everything in her husband's life', but how could he interest her in breaking-strains and weights, cruppers and breastplates? The real clash is between Minnie and work; poking about when he tries to escape her interruptions, she finds a letter from Mrs. Herriott, but since he cares nothing for Mrs. Herriott, that can be dealt with. But when she does whisper her little secret, the harness is forgotten and Minnie has won.

They lose their first child, Minnie has high fever and almost dies but she recovers and a new baby prospers. But Gadsby knows he is ruined as a cavalry officer; he has lost his nerve. He is afraid that he will fall and his squadron will gallop over him. Before his marriage, he had given no more thought to death than to Mrs. Herriott's feelings. He sends in his papers and goes to England to be the squire at his family place.

L'Envoi, the verse epilogue to *The Gadsbys,* explicitly asks: 'What is the moral?' And the answer is unequivocal. 'Red lips tarnish the scabbarded steel... He travels the fastest who travels alone...' or in plain prose: 'A good man married is a good man marred...' This too is a recurrent Kipling theme and it is cynical enough but it is never safe to take Kipling quite literally. He *wanted* married happiness for himself – but he did not want to show it. At the same time, he wanted, as always, to show how grown-up and knowing he was. He had outgrown his own teen-age love for Flo Garrard and he had made friends with at least two charming older women rather like Mrs. Hauksbee who gave him good advice. But in my judgment he did not know much at first hand about love. In nearly all those early writings about flirtations in Simla there is something sentimental because they are about emotions not deeply felt (I except as one example *The Other Man* in Plain Tales.) Everything Gadsby says to Minnie is sentimental, except when she is dying. But these basically sentimental stories are often expressed in cynical terms because above all things he must not seem callow and innocent.

The Story of the Gadsbys is said to be based on a work popular in France at the time, Gyp's *Autour du Mariage,* and there is no doubt that in all Kipling's early writings about officers and their wives – as opposed to his exploration of the lives of Indians and private soldiers – there is a French influence, particularly that of Maupassant. Gadsby himself was modelled on a Captain Beames of the 19th Bengal Lancers, who made a confidant of Kipling when he met a girl he wanted to marry. (But I wonder whether Beames was quite so selfish a man as Gadsby.) It is carefully observed and carefully drawn. The men Kipling met at the Club did talk like that and laugh at a man who was 'caught'. But there is an ambiguity in the way Kipling sets it down, an over-conscious simplicity. He is mocking. 'Lord, what fools these mortals be!' he says with Puck, as he draws the society in which he moved – and yet a part of him agrees with every word of what they say.

What would have pleased him is that Minnie's death bed scene is still moving and that people still find him readable after a hundred years.

Hither Daggons,   PHILIP MASON
Cripplestyle,   May 1986
Alderholt,
Nr. Fordingbridge,
Hampshire.

THE

STORY OF THE GADSBYS

A TALE WITHOUT A PLOT

BY

RUDYARD KIPLING

AUTHOR OF "SOLDIERS THREE, " WEE WILLIE WINKIE," ETC.

———

PUBLISHED BY
MESSRS. A. H. WHEELER & CO.,
ALLAHABAD

WILKINSON'S
ESSENCE OR FLUID EXTRACT OF
RED JAMAICA SARSAPARILLA

Is the only Preparation recognized by the Faculty as a wonderful

PURIFIER OF THE HUMAN BLOOD.

THOSE SUFFERING FROM THE EFFECTS OF TROPICAL CLIMATES,

SUCH AS

Torpid Liver, Debility, Attenuation of the Body, Eruptions, Lassitude, &c.,

WILL BY TAKING THIS

Essence of Red Jamaica Sarsaparilla

Soon find relief, and ultimately a cure. It is asserted by those who take a little daily that the system becomes less liable to attacks of illness of all kinds.

The best remedy against "prickly heat".

"We cannot speak too highly of it."—*Lancet.*

The late Lord Clyde, writing for WILKINSON'S SARSAPARILLA, says: "I am never without it, for, when feeling depressed or out of sorts, from anxiety and fatigue, a dose or two animates me."

"Your Essence of RED JAMAICA SARSAPARILLA cured me of a Torpid Liver when all other remedies failed."—EARL OF ALDBOROUGH.

BEWARE OF IMITATIONS!!!
Which are worthless, and some injurious.

Ask for **Wilkinson's Essence of Red Jamaica Sarsaparilla,** and take no other. The genuine has the Trade Mark as above on the Labels, Wrappers, and Crates.

AGENTS IN ALL THE PRINCIPAL TOWNS OF INDIA.

Established at 270 Regent St., London, W., since 1829.

PREFACE.

To the address of
CAPTAIN J. MAFFLIN,
Duke of Derry's (Pink) Hussars.

Dear Mafflin,

You will remember that I wrote this story as an Awful Warning. None the less you have seen fit to disregard it, and have followed Gadsby's example—as I betted you would. I acknowledge that you paid the money at once, but you have prejudiced the mind of Mrs. Mafflin against myself; for though I am almost the only respectable friend of your bachelor days, she has refused my card to me throughout the season. Further, she caused you to invite me to dinner at the Club, where you called me "a wild ass of the desert," and went home at half-past ten, after discoursing for twenty minutes on the responsibilites of house-keeping. You now drive a mail-phaeton and sit under a Church of England clergyman. I am not angry, Jack. It is your fate, as it was Gaddy's, and his fate who can avoid? Do not think that I am moved by a spirit of revenge as I write, thus publicly, that you and you alone are responsible for this book. In other and more expansive days, when you could look at a magnum without flushing and at a cheroot without turning white, you supplied me with most of the material. Take it back again—would that I could have preserved your fetterless speech in the telling—take it back, and by your slippered hearth read it to the late Miss Deercourt. She will not be any the more willing to receive my cards, but she will admire you immensely, and you, I feel sure, will love me. You may even invite me to another very bad dinner—at the Club, which as you and your wife know, is a safe neutral ground for the entertainment of wild asses. Then, my very dear hypocrite, we shall be quits.

Yours always,

RUDYARD KIPLING.

P.S.—On second thoughts I should recommend you to keep the book away from Mrs. Mafflin.

CONTENTS.

~~~~~~~~~~

POOR DEAR MAMMA.

The wild hawk to the wind-swept sky,
The deer to the wholesome wold,
And the heart of a man to the heart of a maid,
As it was in the days of old.

Gipsy Song.

SCENE.—*Interior of Miss Minnie Threegan's bed-room at Simla. Miss Threegan, in window-seat, turning over a drawerful of Chiffons. Miss Emma Deercourt, bosom-friend who has come to spend the day, sitting on the bed, manipulating the bodice of a ball-room frock and a bunch of artificial Lilies of the Valley. Time 5·30 P.M., on a hot May afternoon.*

MISS DEERCOURT.—And *he* said, " I shall *never* forget this dance," and, of course, I said, " Oh! How *can* you be so silly! " Do you think he meant anything, dear?

MISS THREEGAN (*extracting long lavender silk stockings from the rubbish*).—You know him better than I do.

MISS D.—Oh *do* be sympathetic, Minnie! I'm sure he does. At least I would be sure, if he wasn't always riding with that odious Mrs. Hagan.

MISS T.—I suppose so. How *does* one manage to dance through one's heels first? Look at this—isn't it shameful? (*Spreads stocking-heel on open hand for inspection.*)

MISS D.—Never mind that! You can't mend it. Help me with this hateful bodice. I've run the string *so,* and I've run the string *so,* and I *can't* make the fullness come right. Where would you put this? (*Waves Lilies of the Valley.*)

MISS T.—As high up on the shoulder as possible.

MISS D.—Am I quite tall enough? I know it makes May Olger look lopsided.

MISS T.—Yes, but May hasn't your shoulders. Her's are like a hock-bottle.

BEARER (*rapping at door*).—Captain *Sahib* has come.

MISS D. (*jumping up wildly, and hunting for body which she has discarded owing to the heat of the day*).—Captain *Sahib!* What, Captain *Sahib?* Oh, good gracious, and I'm only half-dressed! Well, I shan't bother.

MISS T. (*calmly*).—You needn't. It isn't for us. That's Captain Gadsby. He is going for a ride with Mamma. He generally comes five days out of the seven.

AGONISED VOICE (*from an inner apartment*).—Minnie, run out and give Captain Gadsby some tea, and tell him I shall be ready in ten minutes; and, O Minnie, come to me an instant, there's a dear girl!

MISS T.—O bother! (*Aloud.*) Very well, Mamma.

Exits and reappears, after five minutes, flushed and rubbing her fingers.

MISS D.—You look pink. What has happened?

MISS T. (*in a stage whisper*).—A twenty-four inch waist, and she won't let it out! Where *are* my bangles? (*Rummages on the toilet table, and dabs at her hair with a brush in the interval.*)

MISS D.—Who is this Captain Gadsby? I don't think I've met him.

MISS T.—You must have. He belongs to the Harrar set. I've danced with him, but I've never talked to him. He's a big yellow man, in the Pink Hussars, just like a newly hatched chicken, with an e-normous moustache. He walks like this (*imitates Cavalry swagger*), and he goes, "Ha-Hmmm!" deep down in his throat, when he can't think of anything to say. Mamma likes him. I don't.

MISS D. (*abstractedly*).—Does he wax that moustache?

MISS T. (*busy with powder-puff*).—Yes, I think so. Why?

MISS D. (*bending over bodice and sewing furiously*).—Oh, nothing—only ——

MISS T. (*sternly*).—Only what? Out with it, Emma.

MISS D.—Well, May Ogler—she's engaged to Mr. Charteris, you know—said . . . . Promise you won't repeat this?

Miss T.—Yes, I promise. What did she say?

Miss D.—That—that being kissed (*with a rush*) by a man who *didn't* wax his moustache was—like eating an egg without salt.

Miss T. (*at her full height, with crushing scorn*).—May Olger is a horrid, nasty *Thing*, and you can tell her I said so. I'm glad she doesn't belong to my set.—I must go and feed this man. Do I look presentable?

Miss D.—Yes, perfectly. Be quick and hand him over to your Mother, and then we can talk. I shall listen at the door to hear what you say to him.

Miss T.—'Sure I don't care. *I'm* not afraid of Captain Gadsby!

In proof of this swings into drawing-room with a mannish stride followed by two short steps, which produces the effect of a restive horse entering. Misses Captain Gadsby, who is sitting in the shadow of the window-curtain, and gazes round helplessly.

Captain Gadsby (*aside*).—The filly, by Jove! Must ha picked up that action from the sire. (*Aloud, rising.*) Good evening, Miss Threegan.

Miss T. (*conscious that she is flushing*).—Good evening, Captain Gadsby. Mamma told me to say that she will be ready in a few minutes. Won't you have some tea? (*Aside.*) I hope Mamma will be quick. What *am* I to say to the creature? (*Aloud and abruptly.*) Milk and sugar?

Captain G.—No sugar tha-anks, and very little milk. Ha-Hmmm.

Miss T. (*aside*).—If he's going to do that, I'm lost. I shall laugh. I *know* I shall!

Captain G. (*pulling at his moustache and watching it sideways down his nose*).—Ha-Hmmm. (*Aside.*) Wonder what the little beast can talk about. Must make a shot at it.

Miss T. (*aside*).—Oh, this is agonising. I *must* say something.

Both Together.—Have you been —— ?

CAPTAIN G.—I beg your pardon. You were going to say—

MISS T. (*who has been watching the moustache with awed fascination*).—Won't you have some eggs ?

CAPTAIN G. (*looking bewilderedly at the tea-table*).—Eggs ! —(*Aside.*) Oh, Hades ! She must have a nursery-tea at this hour. S'pose they've wiped her mouth and sent her to me while the Mother is getting on her duds.—(*Aloud.*) No, thanks.

MISS T. (*crimson with confusion*).—Oh ! I didn't mean that. I wasn't thinking of mou—eggs for an instant. I meant *salt.* Won't you have some sa—sweets ?—(*Aside.*) He'll think me a raving lunatic ! I wish Mamma would come.

CAPTAIN G. (*aside*).—It *was* a nursery-tea and she's ashamed of it. By Jove ! She doesn't look half bad when she colours up like that. (*Aloud, helping himself from the dish.*) Have you seen those new chocolates at Peliti's ?

MISS T.—No, I made these myself. What are they like?

CAPTAIN G.—These ! *De-*licious. (*Aside.*) And that's a fact.

MISS T. (*aside*).—Oh, bother ! He'll think I'm fishing for compliments. (*Aloud.*) No, Peliti's of course.

CAPTAIN G. (*enthusiastically*). — Not to compare with these. How d'you make them. I can't get my man to understand the simplest thing beyond roast mutton and fowl.

MISS T.—Yes ? I'm not a *khansamah,* you know. Perhaps you frighten him. You should never frighten a servant. He loses his head. It's very bad policy.

CAPTAIN G.—He's so awf'ly stupid.

MISS T. (*folding her hands in her lap*).—You should call him quietly and say : " *O khansamah !* "

CAPTAIN G. (*getting interested*). — Yes. (*Aside.*) Fancy that little featherweight saying : " *O khansamah* " to my blood-thirsty Mir Khan !

MISS T.—Then you should explain the dinner dish by dish.

CAPTAIN G.—But I can't speak the vernacular.

Miss T. (*patronisingly*).—You should pass the Higher Standard and try.

Captain G.—I have, but I don't seem to be any the wiser. Are you?

Miss T.—I never passed the Higher Standard. But the butler is very patient with me. He doesn't get angry when I talk about sheep's hats, or order tons of gram when I mean pounds.

Captain G. (*aside, with intense indignation*).—I'd like to see Mir Khan being rude to that girl! Hullo! Steady the Buffs! (*Aloud.*) And do you understand about horses, too?

Miss T.—A little—not very much. I can't doctor them, but I know what they ought to eat, and I am in charge of our stable.

Captain G.—Indeed! You might help me, then. What ought a man to give his groom in the Hills? My ruffian says eight rupees, because everything is so dear.

Miss T.—Six rupees a month, and one rupee Simla allowance—neither more nor less. And a grass-cutter gets six rupees. That's better than buying grass in the bazaar.

Captain G. (*admiringly*).—How do you know?

Miss T.—I have tried both ways.

Captain G.—Do you ride much, then? I've never seen you on the Mall?

Miss T. (*aside*).—I haven't passed him *more* than fifty times. (*Aloud.*) Nearly every day.

Captain G.—By Jove! I didn't know that. Ha-Hmmm! (*Pulls at his moustaches and is silent for forty seconds.*)

Miss T. (*desperately, and wondering what will happen next*).—It looks beautiful. I shouldn't touch it if I were you. (*Aside.*) It's all Mamma's fault for not coming before. I *will* be rude!

Captain G. (*bronzing under the tan, and bringing down his hand very quickly*).—Eh? Wha-at! Oh, yes! Ha! ha! (*Laughs uneasily.*) (*Aside.*) Well, of *all* the dashed cheek! I never had a woman say that to me yet. She must be a cool hand, or else. . . . Ah! that nursery-tea!

VOICE FROM THE UNKNOWN.—Tchk! Tchk! Tchk!

CAPTAIN G.—Good gracious! What's that?

MISS T.—The dog, I think. (*Aside.*) Emma *has* been listening and I'll never forgive her!

CAPTAIN G. (*aside*).—They don't keep dogs here. (*Aloud.*) 'Didn't sound like a dog, did it?

MISS T.—Then it must have been the cat. Let's go into the verandah. What a lovely evening it is!

Steps into verandah and looks out across the hills into sunset. The Captain follows.

CAPTAIN G. (*aside*).—Superb eyes! I wonder that I never noticed them before? (*Aloud.*) There's going to be a dance at Viceregal Lodge on Wednesday. Can you spare me one?

MISS T. (*shortly*).—No! I don't want any of your charity-dances. You only ask me because Mamma told you to. I hop and I bump. You *know* I do!

CAPTAIN G. (*aside*).—That's true, but little girls shouldn't understand these things. (*Aloud.*) No, on my word I don't. You dance beautifully.

MISS T.—Then why do you always stand out after half a dozen turns? I thought officers in the Army didn't tell fibs.

CAPTAIN G.—It wasn't a fib, believe me. I really *do* want the pleasure of a dance with you.

MISS T. (*wickedly*).—Why? Won't Mamma dance with you any more?

CAPTAIN G. (*more earnestly than the necessity demands*).— I wasn't thinking of your Mother. (*Aside.*) You little vixen!

MISS T. (*still looking out of the window*).—Eh? Oh, I beg your pardon. I was thinking of something else.

CAPTAIN G. (*aside*).—Well! I wonder what she'll say next. I've never known a woman treat *me* like this before. I might be—dash it, I might be an Infantry subaltern! (*Aloud.*) Oh, *please* don't trouble. I'm not worth thinking about. Isn't your Mother ready yet?

MISS T.—I should think so; but promise me, Captain Gadsby, you won't take poor dear Mamma for such long rides any more. They tire her so.

CAPTAIN G.—She says that no exercise tires her?

MISS T.—Yes, but she suffers afterwards. *You* don't know what rheumatism is, and you oughtn't to keep her out so late, when it gets chilly in the evenings.

CAPTAIN G. (*aside*).—Rheumatism! I thought she came off her horse rather in a bunch. Whew! One lives and learns. (*Aloud.*) I'm sorry to hear that. She hasn't mentioned it to me.

MISS T. (*flurried*).—Of course not! Poor dear Mamma never would. And you mustn't say that I told you either. Promise me that you won't! Oh, Captain Gadsby, *promise* me you won't!

CAPTAIN G.—I am dumb or—I shall be as soon as you've given me that dance, and another . . . if you can trouble yourself to think about me for a minute.

MISS T.—But you won't like it one little bit. You'll be awfully sorry afterwards.

CAPTAIN G.—I shall like it above all things, and I shall only be sorry that I didn't get more. (*Aside.*) Now what in the world am I saying?

MISS T.—Very well. You will have only yourself to thank if your toes are trodden on. Shall we say Seven?

CAPTAIN G.—And Eleven. (*Aside.*) She can't be more than eight stone, but, even then, it's an absurdly small foot. (*Looks at his own riding boots.*)

MISS T.—They're beautifully shiny. I can almost see my face in them.

CAPTAIN G.—I was thinking whether I should have to go on crutches for the rest of my life if you trod on my toes.

MISS T.—Very likely. Why not change Eleven for a square?

CAPTAIN G.—No, please! I want them both waltzes. Won't you write them down?

MISS T.—*I* don't get so many dances that I shall confuse them. *You* will be the offender.

CAPTAIN G.—Wait and see! (*Aside.*) She doesn't dance perfectly, perhaps, but ——

MISS T.—Your tea must have got cold by this time. Won't you have another cup ?

CAPTAIN G.—No, thanks. Don't you think it's pleasanter out in the verandah? (*Aside.*) I never saw hair take that colour in the sunshine before. (*Aloud.*) It's like one of Dicksee's pictures.

MISS T.—Yes ! It's a wonderful sunset, isn't it ? (*Bluntly.*) But what do *you* know about Dicksee's pictures ?

CAPTAIN G.—I go Home occasionally. And I used to know the Galleries. (*Nervously.*) You mustn't think only a Philistine with—a moustache.

MISS T.—Don't! *Please* don't ! I'm *so* sorry for what I said then. I was *horribly* rude. It slipped out before I thought. Don't you know the temptation to say frightful and shocking things just for the mere sake of saying them ? I'm afraid I gave way to it.

CAPTAIN G. (*watching the girl as she flushes*).—I *think* I know the feeling. It would be terrible if we all yielded to it, wouldn't it ? For instance, I might say ——

POOR DEAR MAMMA (*entering, habited, hatted and booted*). —Ah, Captain Gadsby ! 'Sorry to keep you waiting. 'Hope you hav'n't been bored. My little girl been talking to you ?

MISS T.(*aside*).—I'm not sorry I spoke about the rheumatism. I'm not. I'm NOT ! I only wish I'd mentioned the corns too.

CAPTAIN G. (*aside*).—What a shame ! I wonder how old she is. It never occurred to me before. (*Aloud.*) We've been discussing " Shakespeare and the musical glasses " in the verandah.

MISS. T. (*aside*).—Nice man ! He knows that quotation. He isn't a Philistine, with a moustache. (*Aloud.*) Goodbye, Captain Gadsby. (*Aside.*) What a huge hand, and *what* a squeeze ! I don't suppose he meant it, but he has driven the rings into my fingers.

Poor Dear Mamma.—Has *Vermilion* come round yet?
Oh, yes! Captain Gadsby, don't you think that the saddle
is too far forward? (*They pass into the front verandah.*)
Captain G. (*aside*).—How the dickens should I know
what she prefers? She told me that she doated on horses.
(*Aloud.*) I think it is.

Miss T. (*coming out into front verandah*).—Oh! Bad
Buldoo! I must speak to the boy for this. He has taken
up the curb two links, and *Vermilion* hates that. (*Passes out,
and to horse's head.*)

Captain G.—Let me do it!

Miss T.—No, *Vermilion* understands me. Don't you,
old man? (*Looses curb-chain skilfully, and pats horse on nose
and throttle.*) Poor *Vermilion!* Did they want to cut his
chin off? There!

*Captain Gadsby watches the interlude with undisguised
admiration.*

Poor Dear Mamma (*tartly to Miss T.*).—You've forgotten
your guest, I think, dear.

Miss T.—Good gracious! So I have! Good-bye. (*Retreats indoors hastily.*)

Poor Dear Mamma (*bunching reins in fingers hampered
by too tight gauntlets*).—Captain Gadsby!

Captain Gadsby *stoops, and makes the foot-rest.* Poor
Dear Mamma *blunders, halts too long, and breaks through it.*

Captain G. (*aside*).—Must I hold up eleven stone for
ever? It's all your rheumatism. (*Aloud.*) Can't imagine
why I was so clumsy. (*Aside.*) Now Little Featherweight
would have gone up like a bird.

They ride out of the garden. The Captain falls back.

Captain G. (*aside*).—How that habit catches her under
the arms! Ugh!

Poor Dear Mamma (*with the worn smile of sixteen seasons,
the worse for exchange*).—You're dull this afternoon, Captain
Gadsby.

CAPTAIN G. (*spurring up wearily*).—Why did you keep me waiting so long ?

Et cœtera, et cœtera, et cœtera.

AN INTERVAL OF THREE WEEKS.

GILDED YOUTH (*sitting on railings opposite Simla Town Hall*).—Hullo, Gaddy ! 'Been trotting out the Gorgonzola ? We all thought it was the Gorgon you're mashing.

CAPTAIN G. (*with withering emphasis*).—You young cub ! What the —— does it matter to you ?

Proceeds to read Gilded Youth a lecture on discretion and deportment, which crumples latter like a Chinese lantern. Departs fuming.

FURTHER INTERVAL OF FIVE WEEKS.

SCENE.—*Exterior of New Library on a foggy evening. Miss Threegan and Miss Deercourt meet among the 'rickshaws. Miss T. is carrying a bundle of books under her left arm.*

MISS D. (*level intonation*).—Well ?

MISS T. (*ascending intonation*).—Well ?

MISS D. (*capturing her friend's left arm, taking away all the books, placing books in 'rickshaw, returning to arm, securing hand by the third finger and investigating*).—Well ! You *bad* girl ! And you *never* told me.

MISS T. (*demurely*).—He—he—he only spoke yesterday afternoon.

MISS D.—Bless you, dear ! And I'm to be bridesmaid, aren't I ? You know you promised *ever* so long ago.

MISS T.—Of course. I'll tell you all about it to-morrow. (*Gets into 'rickshaw.*) Oh, Emma !

MISS D. (*with intense interest*).—Yes, dear.

MISS T. (*piano*).—It's quite true—about—the—egg.

MISS D.—What egg ?

MISS T. (*pianissimo prestissimo*).—The egg without the salt. (*Forte.*) *Chalo ghar ko jaldi, jhampani !*

CURTAIN.

THE WORLD WITHOUT.

"Certain people of importance."

SCENE—*Smoking Room of the Degchi Club. Time 10·30 p.m. of a stuffy night in the Rains. Four men dispersed in picturesque attitudes and easy chairs. To these enter Blayne of the Irregular Moguls, in evening dress.*

BLAYNE.—Phew! The Judge ought to be hanged in his own store-godown. Hi, boy! Strong whisky-peg, to take the taste out of my mouth.

CURTISS (*Royal Artillery*).—That's it, is it? What the deuce made you dine at the Judge's? You know his cookery.

BLAYNE.—'Thought it couldn't be worse than the Club; but I'll swear he buys ullaged liquor and doctors it with gin and ink (*looking round the room*). Is this all of you to-night?

DOONE (*P. W. D.*).—Anthony was called out at dinner. Mingle had a pain in his tummy.

CURTISS.—Miggy dies of cholera once a week in the Rains, and gets drunk on chlorodyne in between. 'Good little chap, though. Anyone at the Judge's, Blayne?

BLAYNE.—Cockley and his wife, looking awfully white and fagged. 'Female girl—couldn't catch the name—on her way to the Hills, under the Cockley's charge—the Judge, and Markyn fresh from Simla—disgustingly fit.

CURTISS.—Good Lord, how truly magnificent! Was there enough ice? When I mangled garbage there I got one whole lump—nearly as big as a walnut. What had Markyn to say for himself?

BLAYNE.—'Seems that everyone is having a fairly good time up there, in spite of the rain. By Jove, that reminds me! I know I hadn't come across just for the pleasure of your society. News! Great news! Markyn told me.

DOONE.—Who's dead now?

BLAYNE.—No one that I know of; but Gaddy's hooked at last!

DROPPING CHORUS.—How much? The Devil! Markyn was pulling your leg. Not GADDY!

BLAYNE.—It's been given out up above.

MACKESY (*Barrister-at-law*).—Huh! Women will give out anything. What does accused say?

BLAYNE.—Markyn told me that he congratulated him warily—one hand held out, t'other ready to guard. Gaddy turned pink and said it was so.

CURTISS.—Poor old Gaddy! They all do it. Who's *she?* Let's hear the details.

BLAYNE.—She's a girl—daughter of a Colonel Somebody.

DOONE.—Simla's stiff with Colonels' daughters. Be more explicit.

BLAYNE.—Wait a shake. What was her name? Three—something. Three—

CURTISS.—Stars, perhaps. Gaddy knows *that* brand.

BLAYNE.—Threegan—Minnie Threegan.

MACKESY.—Threegan! Isn't she a little bit of a girl with red hair?

BLAYNE.—'Bout that—from what Markyn said.

MACKESY.—Then I've met her. She was at Lucknow last season. 'Owned a permanently juvenile Mamma, and danced damnably. I say, Jervoise, you knew the Threegans, didn't you?

JERVOISE (*Civilian of twenty-five years' service, waking up from his doze*).—Eh! What's that? Knew who? How? I thought I was at home, confound you!

MACKESY.—The Threegan girl's engaged, so Blayne says.

JERVOISE (*slowly*).—Engaged—engaged! Bless my soul, I'm getting an old man! Little Minnie Threegan engaged! It was only the other day I went home with them in the *Surat*—no, the *Massilia*—and she was crawling about on her hands and knees among the ayahs. 'Used to call me "The

Tick Tack *Sahib*" because I showed her my watch. And that was in 'Sixty-Seven or 'Seventy. Good God, how time flies! I'm an old man. I remember when Threegan married Miss Derwent—daughter of old Hooky Derwent—but that was before your time. And so the little baby's engaged to have a little baby of her own! Who's the other fool?

MACKESY.—Gadsby of the Pink Hussars.

JERVOISE.—'Never met him. Threegan lived in debt, married in debt, and 'll die in debt. 'Must be glad to get the girl off his hands.

BLAYNE.—Gaddy has money—lucky devil. Place at home, too.

DOONE.—He comes of first-class stock. 'Can't quite understand his being caught by a Colonel's daughter, and (*looking cautiously round room*) Black Infantry at that! No offence to you, Blayne.

BLAYNE (*stiffly*).—Not much, tha-anks.

CURTISS (*quoting motto of Irregular Moguls*).—"We are what we are," eh, old man? But Gaddy was such a superior animal as a rule. Why didn't he go home and pick his wife there?

MACKESY.—They are all alike when they come to the turn into the straight. About thirty a man begins to get sick of living alone—

CURTISS.—And of the eternal mutton-chop in the morning.

DOONE.—It's dead goat as a rule, but go on, Mackesy.

MACKESY.—If a man's once taken that way nothing will hold him. Do you remember Benoit of your service, Doone? They transferred him to Tharanda when his time came, and he married a platelayer's daughter or something of that kind. She was the only female about the place.

DOONE.—Yes, poor brute. That smashed Benoit's chances altogether. Mrs. Benoit used to ask :—"Was you goin' to the dance this evenin'?"

CURTISS.—Hang it all! Gaddy hasn't married beneath him. There's no dark blood in the family, I suppose.

JERVOISE.—Tar-brush! Not an ounce. You young fellows talk as though the man was doing the girl an honour in marrying her. You're all too conceited—nothing's good enough for you.

BLAYNE.—Not even an empty Club, a dam' bad dinner at the Judge's, and a Station as sickly as a hospital. You're quite right. We're a set of Sybarites.

DOONE.—Luxurious dogs, wallowing in ——

CURTISS.—Prickly-heat between the shoulders. I'm covered with it. Let's hope Beora will be cooler.

BLAYNE.—Whew! Are *you* ordered into camp, too? I thought the Gunners had a clean cholera sheet.

CURTISS.—No, worse luck. Two cases yesterday—one died—and if we have a third, out we go. Is there any shooting at Beora, Doone?

DOONE.—The country's under water, except the patch by the Grand Trunk Road. I was there yesterday, looking at a dam, and came across four poor devils of natives in their last stage. It's rather bad from here to Kuchara.

CURTISS.—Then we're pretty certain to have a heavy attack. Heigho! I shouldn't mind changing places with Gaddy for a while. 'Sport with Amaryllis in the shade of the Town Hall, and all that. Oh, why doesn't somebody come and marry me, instead of letting me go into cholera camp?

MACKESY—Give us a little peace. If they followed you here I'd resign—on moral grounds.

CURTISS.—You irreclaimable ruffian! You'll stand me another drink for that. Blayne, what will you take? Mackesy is fined—on moral grounds. Doone, have you any preference?

DOONE.—Small glass Kummel, please. Excellent carminative, these days. Anthony told me so.

MACKESY (*signing voucher for four drinks*).—Most unfair punishment. I only thought of Curtiss as Actæon being chevied round the billiard-tables by the nymphs of Diana.

BLAYNE.—Curtiss would have to import his nymphs by train. Mrs. Cockley's the only woman in the Station. She won't leave Cockley, and he's doing his best to get her to go.

CURTISS.—Good, indeed! Here's Mrs. Cockley's health. To the only wife in the Station and a thundering brave woman!

OMNES (*drinking*).—A thundering brave woman!

BLAYNE.—I suppose Gaddy will bring his wife here at the end of the cold weather. They are going to be married almost immediately, I believe.

CURTISS.—Gaddy may thank his luck that the Pink Hussars are all detachment and no head-quarters this hot weather, or he'd be torn from the arms of his love as sure as death. Have you ever noticed the thorough-minded way British Cavalry take to cholera? It's because they are so expensive. If the Pinks had stood fast here, they would have been out in camp a month ago. Yes, I should decidedly like to be Gaddy.

MACKESY.—He'll go Home after he's married, and send in his papers—see if he doesn't.

BLAYNE.—Why shouldn't he? Hasn't he money? Would any one of us be here if we weren't paupers?

DOONE.—Poor old pauper! What has become of the six hundred you rooked from our table last month?

BLAYNE.—It took unto itself wings. I think an enterprising tradesman got some of it, and a money lender gobbled the rest—or else I spent it.

CURTISS.—Gaddy never had dealings with a money lender in his life.

DOONE.—Virtuous Gaddy! If *I* had three thousand a month, paid from England, I don't think I'd borrow either.

MACKESY (*yawning*).—Oh, it's a sweet life! I wonder whether matrimony would make it sweeter.

CURTISS.—Ask Cockley—with his wife dying by inches!

BLAYNE.—Go Home and get a fool of a girl to come out to—what is it Thackeray says?—"the splendid palace of an Indian pro-consul".

DOONE.—Which reminds me. My quarters leak like a sieve. I had fever last night from sleeping in a swamp. And the worst of it is, one can't do anything to a roof till the Rains are over.

CURTISS.—What's wrong with you? *You* haven't eighty rotting soldiers to take into a running stream.

DOONE.—No; but I'm a compost of boils and bad language. I'm a regular Job all over my body. It's sheer poverty of blood, and I don't see any chance of getting richer —either way.

BLAYNE—Can't you take leave?

DOONE.—That's the pull you Army men have over us. Ten days are nothing in your sight. I'm so important that Government can't find a substitute if I go away. Ye-es, I'd like to be Gaddy, whoever his wife may be.

CURTISS.—You've passed the turn of life that Mackesy was speaking of.

DOONE.—Indeed I have, but I never yet had the brutality to ask a woman to share my life out here.

BLAYNE.—On my soul I believe you're right. I'm thinking of Mrs. Cockley. The woman's an absolute wreck.

DOONE.—Exactly. Because she stays down here. The only way to keep her fit would be to send her to the Hills for eight months—and the same with any woman. I fancy I see myself taking a wife on those terms.

MACKESY.—With the rupee at one and sixpence. The little Doones would be little Dehra Doones, with a fine Mussoorie accent to bring home for the holidays.

DOONE.—Yes, it's an enchanting prospect. By the way, the rupee hasn't done falling yet. The time will come when we shall think ourselves lucky if we only lose half our pay.

CURTISS.—Surely a third's loss enough. Who gains by the arrangement? That's what I want to know.

BLAYNE.—The Silver Question! I'm going to bed if

you begin squabbling. Thank goodness, here's Anthony—looking like a Ghost.

Enter Anthony, Indian Medical Staff, very white and tired.

ANTHONY.—'Evening, Blayne. It's raining in sheets. Get me a wisky-peg, boy. The roads are something ghastly.

CURTISS.—How's Mingle?

ANTHONY.—Very bad, and more frightened. I handed him over to Fewton. Mingle might just as well have called him in the first place, instead of bothering me.

BLAYNE.—He's a nervous little chap. What has he got this time?

ANTHONY.—'Can't quite say. A very bad tummy and a blue funk so far. He asked me at once if it was cholera, and I told him not to be a fool. That soothed him.

CURTISS.—Poor devil! The funk does half the business in a man of that build.

ANTHONY (*lighting a cheroot*).—I firmly believe the funk will kill him if he stays down. You know the amount of trouble he's been giving Fewton for the last three weeks. He's doing his very best to frighten himself into the grave.

GENERAL CHORUS.—Poor little devil! Why doesn't he get away?

ANTHONY.—Can't. He has his leave all right, but he's so dipped he can't take it, and I don't think his name on paper would raise four annas. That's in confidence, though.

MACKESY.—All the Station knows it.

ANTHONY.—" I suppose I shall have to die here," he said, squirming all across the bed. He's quite made up his mind to Kingdom Come. And I know he has nothing more than a wet weather tummy if he could only keep a hand on himself.

BLAYNE.—That's bad. That's *very* bad. Poor little Miggy. Good little chap, too. I say—

ANTHONY.—What do you say?

BLAYNE.—Well, look here—anyhow. If it's like that—as you say—I say fifty.

CURTISS.—I say fifty.

MACKESY.—I go twenty better.

DOONE.—Bloated Crœsus of the Bar! I say fifty. Jervoise, what do you say? Hi! Wake up!

JERVOISE.—Eh! What's that? What's that?

CURTISS.—We want a hundred rupees from you. You're a bachelor drawing a gigantic income, and there's a man in a hole.

JERVOISE.—What man? Any one dead?

BLAYNE.—No, but he'll die if you don't give the hundred. Here! Here's a peg-voucher. You can see what we've signed for, and a man will come round to-morrow to collect it. So there will be no trouble.

JERVOISE (*signing*).—One hundred, E. M. J. There you are. It isn't one of your jokes, is it?

BLAYNE.—No; it really *is* wanted. Anthony, you were the biggest poker-winner last week, and you've defrauded the tax-collector too long. Sign!

ANTHONY —Let's see. Three fifties and a seventy—two twenty—three twenty—say four twenty. That'll give him a month clear at the Hills. Many thanks, you men. I'll send round the man to-morrow.

CURTISS.—You must engineer his taking the stuff, and of course you mustn't ——

ANTHONY.—*Of* course. It would never do. He'd weep with gratitude over his evening drink.

BLAYNE.—That's just what he would do, confound him. Oh! I say, Anthony, you pretend to know everything. Have you heard about Gaddy?

ANTHONY.—No. Divorce Court at last?

BLAYNE.—Worse. He's engaged.

ANTHONY.—How much! He *can't* be!

BLAYNE.—He is. He's going to be married in a few weeks. Markyn told me at the Judge's this evening. It's settled.

ANTHONY.—You don't say so? Holy Moses! There'll be a shine in the tents of Kedar.

CURTISS.—Regiment cut up rough, think you ?

ANTHONY.—Don't know anything about the regiment.

MACKESY.—Is it bigamy, then ?

ANTHONY.—May be. Do you mean to say that you men have forgotten, or is there more charity in the world than I thought ?

DOONE.—You don't look pretty when you are trying to keep a secret. You bloat. Explain.

ANTHONY.—Mrs. Herriott !

BLAYNE (*after a long pause, to the room generally*).—It's my notion that we are a set of fools.

MACKESY.—Nonsense. *That* business was knocked on the head last season. Why, young Mallard ——

ANTHONY.—Mallard was a candle-stick, paraded as such. Think a while. Recollect last season, and the talk then. Mallard or no Mallard, did Gaddy ever talk to any other woman ?

CURTISS.—There's something in that. It was slightly noticeable now you come to mention it. But she's at Naini Tal, and he's at Simla.

ANTHONY.—He had to go to Simla to look after a globe-trotter relative of his—a person with a title. Uncle or aunt.

BLAYNE.—And there he got engaged. No law prevents a man growing tired of a woman.

ANTHONY.—Except that he mustn't do it till the woman is tired of him. And the Herriott woman was not that.

CURTISS.—She may be now. Two months of Naini Tal work wonders.

DOONE.—Curious thing how some women carry a Fate with them. There was a Mrs. Deegie in the Central Provinces whose men invariably fell away and got married. It became a regular proverb with us when I was down there. I remember three men desperately devoted to her, and they all, one after another, took wives.

CURTISS.—That's odd. Now I should have thought that

Mrs. Deegie's influence would have led them to take other men's wives. It ought to have made them afraid of the judgment of Providence.

ANTHONY.—Mrs. Herriott will make Gaddy afraid of something more than the judgment of Providence, I fancy.

BLAYNE.—Supposing things are as you say, he'll be a fool to face her. He'll sit tight at Simla.

ANTHONY.—'Shouldn't be a bit surprised if he went off to Naini to explain. He's an unaccountable sort of man, and she's likely to be a more than unaccountable woman.

DOONE.—What makes you take her character away so confidently?

ANTHONY.—*Primum tempus.* Gaddy was her first, and a woman doesn't allow her first man to drop away without expostulation. She justifies the first transfer of affection to herself by swearing that it is for ever and ever. Consequently ——

BLAYNE.—Consequently, we are sitting here till past one o'clock, talking scandal like a set of Station cats. Anthony, it's all your fault. We were perfectly respectable till you came in. Go to bed. I'm off. Good-night all.

CURTISS.—Past one! It's past two by Jove, and here's the man coming for the past closing time charge. Just Heavens! One, two, three, four, *five* rupees to pay for the pleasure of saying that a poor little beast of a woman is no better than she should be. I'm ashamed of myself. Go to bed, you slanderous villains, and if I'm sent to Beora to-morrow, be prepared to hear I'm dead before paying my card-account!

CURTAIN.

THE TENTS OF KEDAR.

SCENE.—*A Naini Tal dinner for thirty-four. Plate, wines, crockery, and service carefully calculated to scale of Rs. 6000 per mensem, less Exchange. Table split lengthways by bank of flowers.*

MRS. HERRIOTT (*after conversation has risen to proper pitch*).—Ah! 'didn't see you in the crush in the drawing-room. (*Sotto voce.*) Where *have* you been all this while, Pip?

CAPTAIN GADSBY (*turning from regularly ordained dinner partner and settling glasses*).—Good evening. (*Sotto voce.*) Not quite so loud another time. You've no notion how your voice carries. (*Aside.*) So much for shirking the written explanation. It'll have to be a verbal one now. Sweet prospect! How on earth am I to tell her that I am a respectable, engaged member of society, and it's all over between us?

MRS. H.—I've a heavy score against you. Where were you at the Monday Pop? Where were you on Tuesday? Where were you at the Lamont's tennis. I was looking everywhere.

CAPTAIN G.—For me! Oh, I was alive somewhere, I suppose. (*Aside.*) It's for Minnie's sake, but it's going to be dashed unpleasant.

MRS. H.—Have I done anything to offend you? I never meant it if I have. I couldn't help going for a ride with the Vaynor man. It was promised a week before you came up.

CAPTAIN G.—I didn't know ——

MRS. H.—It really *was.*

CAPTAIN G.—Auything about it, I mean.

MRS. H.—What has upset you to-day ? All these days? You haven't been near me for four whole days—nearly one hundred hours. Was it *kind* of you, Pip ? And I've been looking forward so much to your coming.

CAPTAIN G.—Have you ?

MRS. H.—You know I have ! I've been as foolish as a school-girl about it. I made a little calendar and put it in my card-case, and every time the twelve o'clock gun went off I scratched out a square and said : " That brings me nearer to Pip. *My* Pip."

CAPTAIN G. (*with an uneasy laugh*).—What will Mackler think if you neglect him so ?

MRS. H.—And it hasn't brought you nearer. You seem farther away than ever. Are you sulking about something ? I know your temper.

CAPTAIN G.—No.

MRS. H.—Have I grown old in the last few months, then? (*Reaches forward to bank of flowers for menu-card.*)

PARTNER ON LEFT.—Allow me. (*Hands menu-card. Mrs. H. keeps her arm at full stretch for three seconds.*)

MRS. H. (*To partner*).—Oh, thanks. I didn't see. (*Turns right again.*) Is anything in me changed at all ?

CAPTAIN G.—For goodness' sake go on with your dinner ! You must eat something. Try one of those cutlet arrangements. (*Aside.*) And I fancied she had good shoulders, once upon a time ! What a fool a man can make of himself !

MRS. H. (*helping herself to a paper frill, seven peas, some stamped carrots, and a spoonful of gravy*).—That isn't an answer. Tell me whether I have done anything.

CAPTAIN G. (*aside*).—If it isn't ended here there will be a ghastly scene somewhere else. If only I'd written to her and stood the racket—at long range ! (*To butler.*) Yes, Champagne. (*Aloud.*) I'll tell you later on.

Mrs. H.—Tell me *now.* It must be some foolish mis-understanding, and you know that there was to be nothing of that sort between us? *We,* of all people in the world, can't afford it. Is it the Vaynor man, and don't you like to say so? On my honour ——

Captain G.—I haven't given the Vaynor man a thought.

Mrs. H.—But how d'you know that *I* haven't?

Captain G. (*aside*).—Here's my chance, and may the Devil help me through with it. (*Aloud and measuredly.*) Believe me, I do not care how often or how tenderly you think of the Vaynor man.

Mrs. H.—I wonder if you mean that—oh, what *is* the good of squabbling and pretending to misunderstand when you are only up for so short a time? Pip, don't be a stupid!

Follows a pause, during which he crosses his left leg over his right and continues his dinner.

Captain G. (*in answer to the thunderstorm in her eyes*).—Corns—my worst.

Mrs. H.—Upon my word, you are the very rudest man in the world! I'll never do it again.

Captain G. (*aside*).—No, I don't think you will; but I wonder what you will do before it's all over. (*To butler.*) More Champagne, please.

Mrs. H.—Well! Haven't you the grace to apologise, bad man?

Captain G. (*aside*).—I mustn't let it drift back *now.* Trust a woman for being as blind as a bat when she won't see.

Mrs. H.—I'm waiting; or would you like me to dictate a form of apology?

Captain. G. (*desperately*).—By all means dictate.

Mrs. H. (*lightly*).—Very well. Rehearse your several Christian names after me and go on:—" Profess my sincere repentance ".

Captain G.--" Sincere repentance."

Mrs. H.—" For having behaved—— "

CAPTAIN G. (*aside*).—At last! I wish to goodness she'd look away. "For having behaved"—as I have behaved, and declare that I am thoroughly and heartily sick of the whole business, and take this opportunity of making clear my intention of ending it, now, henceforward, and for ever. (*Aside.*) If anyone had told me I should be such a blackguard! . . .

MRS. H. (*shaking a spoonful of potato-chips into her plate*). —That's not a pretty joke.

CAPTAIN G.—No. It's a reality. (*Aside.*) I wonder if smashes of this kind are always so raw.

MRS. H.—Really, Pip, you're getting more absurd every day.

CAPTAIN G.—I don't think you quite understand me. Shall I repeat it?

MRS. H.—No! For pity's sake, don't do that. It's too terrible, even in fun.

CAPTAIN G. (*aside*).—I'll let her think it over for a while. But I ought to be horse-whipped.

MRS. H.—I want to know what you meant by what you said just now.

CAPTAIN G.—Exactly what I said. No less.

MRS. H.—But what have I done to deserve it? What *have* I done?

CAPTAIN G. (*aside*).—If she only wouldn't look at me (*Aloud and very slowly, his eyes on his plate.*) D'you remember that evening in July, before the Rains broke, when you said that the end would have to come sooner or later, and you wondered for which of us it would come first?

MRS. H.—Yes. I was only joking. And you swore that as long as there was breath in your body it should *never* come. And I believed you.

CAPTAIN G. (*fingering menu-card*).—Well, it has; that's all.

A long pause, during which Mrs. H. bows her head and rolls the bread-twist into little pellets; G. stares at the oleanders.

MRS. H. (*throwing back her head and laughing naturally*). They train us women well, don't they, Pip?

CAPTAIN G. (*brutally, touching shirt stud*).—So far as the expression goes. (*Aside.*) It isn't in her nature to take things quietly. There'll be an explosion yet.

MRS. H. (*with a shudder*).—Thank you. B-but Red Indians allow people to wriggle when they're being tortured, I believe. (*Slips fan from girdle, and fans slowly; rim of fan level with chin.*)

PARTNER ON LEFT.—Very close to-night, isn't it? 'You find it too much for you?

MRS. H.—Oh, no! not in the least. But they really ought to have punkahs, even in your cool Naini Tal, oughtn't they? (*Turns, dropping fan and raising eyebrows.*)

CAPTAIN G.—It's all right. (*Aside.*) Here comes the storm.

MRS. H. (*her eyes on the table-cloth; fan ready in right hand*).—It was very cleverly managed, Pip; and I congratulate you. You swore—you never contented yourself with merely saying a thing—you *swore* that, as far as lay in your power, you'd make my wretched life pleasant for me. And you've denied me the consolation of breaking down. I should have done it—indeed, I should. A woman would hardly have thought of this refinement, my kind, considerate friend. (*Fan-guard, as before.*) You have explained things so tenderly and truthfully, too! You haven't spoken or written a word of warning, and you have let me believe in you till the last minute. You haven't condescended to give me your *reason* yet. No! A woman could not have managed it half so well. Are there many *men* like you in the world?

CAPTAIN G.—I'm sure I don't know. (*To butler.*) Ohé! Champagne.

MRS. H.—You call yourself a man of the world, don't you? Do men of the world behave like Devils when they do a woman the honour to get tired of her?

CAPTAIN G.—I'm sure I don't know. Don't speak so loud.

MRS. H.—Keep us respectable, O Lord, whatever happens! Don't be afraid of my compromising you. You've chosen your ground far too well, and I've been properly brought up. (*Lowering fan.*) Haven't you *any* pity, Pip, except for yourself?

CAPTAIN G.—Wouldn't it be rather impertinent of me to say that I'm sorry for you?

MRS. H.—I think you have said it once or twice before. You're growing very careful of my feelings. Pip, I was a good woman once! You *said* I was. You've made me what I am. What are you going to do with me? What are you going to do with me? Won't you *say* that you are sorry? (*Helps herself to iced asparagus.*)

CAPTAIN G.—I am sorry for you, if you want the pity of such a brute as I am. I'm *awf'ly* sorry for you.

MRS. H.—Rather tame for a man of the world. Do you think that that admission clears you?

CAPTAIN G.—What can I do? I can only tell you what I think of myself. You can't think worse than that?

MRS. H.—Oh, yes, I can. And, now, will you tell me the reason of all this? Remorse? Has Bayard been suddenly conscience-stricken?

CAPTAIN G. (*angrily, his eyes still lowered*).—No! The thing has come to an end on my side. That's all. Done with.

MRS. H.—"That's all. Done with!" As though I were a Cairene Dragoman. You used to make prettier speeches. D'you remember when you said ——

CAPTAIN G.—For heaven's sake, don't bring that ba k! Call me anything you like, and I'll admit it ——

MRS. H.—But you don't care to be reminded of old lies? If I could hope to hurt you one-tenth as much as you have hurt me to-night . . . No, I wouldn't—I couldn't do it, liar though you are.

CAPTAIN G.—I've spoken the truth.

MRS. H.—My *dear* sir, you flatter yourself. You have lied over the reason. Pip, remember that I know you as you don't know yourself. You have been everything to me, though you are . . . (*Fan-guard.*) Oh, what a contemptible *thing* it is! And so you are merely tired of me?

CAPTAIN G.—Since you insist upon my repeating it—Yes.

MRS. H.—Lie the first. I wish I knew a coarser word. Lie seems so ineffectual in your case. The fire has just died out, and there is no fresh one? Think for a minute, Pip, if you care whether I despise you more than I do. Simply *Majisch*, is it?

CAPTAIN G.—Yes. (*Aside.*) I think I deserve this. (*To butler.*) Champagne.

MRS. H.—Lie number two. Before the next glass chokes you, tell me her name.

CAPTAIN G. (*aside*).—I'll make her pay for dragging Minnie into the business. (*Aloud.*) Is it likely?

MRS. H.—*Very* likely, if you thought that it would flatter your vanity. You'd cry my name on the housetops to make people turn round.

CAPTAIN G.—I wish I had. There would have been an end of this business.

MRS. H.—Oh, no, there would not . . . And so you were going to be virtuous and *blasé*, were you? To come to me and say: "I've done with you. The incident is clo-osed." I ought to be proud of having kept such a man so long.

CAPTAIN G. (*aside*).—It only remains to pray for the end of the dinner. (*Aloud.*) You know what I think of myself.

MRS. H.—As it's the only person in the world you ever *do* think of, and as I know your mind thoroughly—I do. You want to get it all over, and . . . Oh, I can't keep you back! And you're going—think of it, Pip—to throw me over for another woman. And you swore that all other women were . . . Pip, my Pip! She *can't* care for you as I do. Believe me, she can't! Is it anyone that I know?"

CAPTAIN G.—Thank goodness it isn't. (*Aside.*) I expected a cyclone, but not an earthquake.

MRS. H.—She *can't*! Is there anything that I wouldn't do for you . . . or haven't done? And to think that I should take this trouble over you, knowing what you are! Do you despise me for it?

Captain G. (*wiping his mouth to hide a smile*).—*Again?* It's entirely a work of charity on your part.

Mrs. H.—Ahhh! But I have no right to resent it . . . Is she better looking than I? Who was it said ——?

Captain G.—No—not that!

Mrs. H.—I'll be more merciful than you were. Don't you know that all women are alike?

Captain G. (*aside*).—Then this is the exception that proves the rule.

Mrs. H.—*All* of them! I'll tell you anything you like. I will, upon my word. They only want the admiration —from anybody—no matter who—anybody! But there is always *one* man that they care for more than any one else in the world, and would sacrifice all the others to. Oh, *do* listen! I've kept the Vaynor man trotting after me like a poodle, and he believes that he is the only man I am interested in. I'll tell you what he said to me.

Captain G.—Spare him. (*Aside.*) I wonder what his version is.

Mrs. H.—He's been waiting for me to look at him all through dinner. Shall I do it, and you can see what an idiot he looks?

Captain G.—"But what imports the nomination of this gentleman?"

Mrs. H.—Watch! (*Sends a glance to the Vaynor man, who tries vainly to combine a mouthful of ice-pudding, a smirk of self-satisfaction, a glare of intense devotion and the stolidity of a British dining countenance.*)

Captain G. (*critically*).—He doesn't look pretty. Why didn't you wait till the spoon was out of his mouth?

Mrs. H.—To amuse you. She'll make an exhibition of you as I've made of him; and people will laugh at you. O, Pip, can't you *see* that? It's as plain as the noonday sun. You'll be trotted about and told lies, and made a fool of like the others. *I* never made a fool of you, did I?

Captain G. (*aside*).—What a clever little woman it is!

Mrs. H.—Well, what have you to say ?

Captain G.—I feel better.

Mrs. H.—Yes, I suppose so, after I have come down to your level. I couldn't have done it if I hadn't cared for you so much. I have spoken the truth.

Captain G.—It doesn't alter the situation.

Mrs. H. (*passionately*).—Then she *has* said that she cares for you! Don't believe her, Pip. It's a lie—as black as yours to me!

Captain G.—Ssssteady! I've a notion that a friend of yours is looking at you.

Mrs. H.—He! I *hate* him. He introduced you to me.

Captain G. (*aside*).—And some people would like women to assist in making the laws. Introduction to imply condonement. (*Aloud.*) Well, you see, if you can remember so far back as that, I couldn't, in common politeness, refuse the offer.

Mrs H.—In common politeness! We have got beyond *that !*

Captain G. (*aside*).—Old ground means fresh trouble. (*Aloud.*) On my honour ——

Mrs. H.—Your *what ?* Ha, ha !

Captain G.—Dishonour, then. She's not what you imagine. I meant to ——

Mrs. H.—Don't tell me anything about her ! She *won't* care for you ; and, when you come back, after having made an exhibition of yourself, you'll find me occupied with ——

Captain G. (*insolently*).—You couldn't while I am alive. (*Aside.*) If that doesn't bring her pride to her rescue, nothing will.

Mrs. H. (*drawing herself up*).—Couldn't do it ? *I ?* (*Softening.*) You're right. I don't believe I could—though you are what you are—a coward and a liar in grain.

Captain G.—It doesn't hurt so much after your little lecture—with demonstrations.

Mrs. H.—One mass of vanity ! Will nothing ever touch

you in this life? There must be a Hereafter if it's only for the benefit of—but you will have it all to yourself.

CAPTAIN G. (*under his eyebrows*).—Are you so certain of that?

MRS. H.—I shall have had mine in this life; and it will serve me right.

CAPTAIN G.—But the admiration that you insisted on so strongly a moment ago? (*Aside.*) Oh, I *am* a brute!

MRS. H. (*fiercely*).—Will that console me for knowing that you will go to her with the same words, the same arguments and the—the same pet names you used to me? And if she cares for you, you two will laugh over my story. Won't that be punishment heavy enough even for me—even for me? . . . And it's all useless. That's another punishment.

CAPTAIN G. (*feebly*).—Oh, come! I'm not so low as you think.

MRS. H.—Not now, perhaps, but you will be. O Pip, if a woman flatters your vanity, there's nothing on earth that you would not tell her; and no meanness that you would not commit. Have I known you so long without knowing that?

CAPTAIN G.—If you can trust me in nothing else—and I don't see why I should be trusted—you can count upon my holding my tongue.

MRS. H.—If you denied everything you've said this evening, and declared it was all in fun (*a long pause*), I'd trust you. Not otherwise. All I ask is, don't tell her my name. *Please* don't. A man might forget: a woman never would. (*Looks up table and sees hostess beginning to collect eyes.*) So it's all ended, through no fault of mine.—Haven't I behaved beautifully? I've accepted your dismissal, and you managed it as cruelly as you could, and I have made you respect my sex, haven't I? (*Arranging gloves and fan.*) I only pray that she'll know you some day as I know you now. I wouldn't be you then, for I think even your conceit will be hurt. I hope she'll pay you back the humiliation you've brought on me. I hope—No. I don't. I *can't* give you up ! I must have something to look forward to, or I shall go crazy. When it's all over, come back to me, come back to me, and you'll find that you're my Pip still !

CAPTAIN G. (*very clearly*).—False move, and you pay for it. It's a girl !

MRS. H. (*rising*).—Then it *was* true ! They said—but I wouldn't insult you by asking. A girl ? *I* was a girl not very long ago. Be good to her, Pip. I dare say she believes in you.

Goes out with an uncertain smile. He watches her through the door, and settles into a chair as the men redistribute themselves.

CAPTAIN G.—Now, if there is any Power who looks after this world, will He kindly tell me what I have done ? (*Reaching out for the claret, and half aloud.*) What *have* I done ?

CURTAIN.

WITH ANY AMAZEMENT.

" And are not afraid with any amazement."

Marriage Service.

SCENE.—*A bachelor's bed-room ; toilet-table arranged with unnatural neatness. Captain Gadsby asleep and snoring heavily. Time,* 10·30 A.M.—*a glorious autumn day at Simla. Enter delicately Captain Mafflin of Gadsby's regiment. Looks at sleeper, and shakes his head murmuring "Poor Gaddy". Performs violent fantasia with hairbrushes on chair-back.*

CAPTAIN M.—Wake up, my sleeping beauty ! (*Howls.*)
" Uprouse ye, then, my merry, merry men !
" It is our opening day !
" It is our opening da-ay ! "
Gaddy, the little dicky-birds have been billing and cooing for ever so long ; and I'm here !

CAPTAIN G. (*sitting up and yawning*).—'Mornin'. This is awf'ly good of you, old fellow. Most awf'ly good of you. Don't know what I should do without you. 'Pon my soul, I don't. 'Haven't slept a wink all night.

CAPTAIN M.—I didn't get in till half-past eleven. 'Had a look at you then, and you seemed to be sleeping as soundly as a condemned criminal.

CAPTAIN G.—Jack, if you want to make those disgustingly worn-out jokes, you'd better go away. (*With portentous gravity.*) It's the happiest day in my life.

CAPTAIN M. (*chuckling grimly*).—Not by a very long chalk, my son. You're going through some of the most refined torture you've ever known. But be calm. *I* am with you. 'Shun ! *Dress !*

CAPTAIN G.—Eh ! Wha-at ?

CAPTAIN M.—*Do* you suppose that you are your own master for the next twelve hours ? If you *do*, of course . . . (*Makes for the door.*)

CAPTAIN G.—No! For goodness sake, old man, don't do that! You'll see me through, wont't you? I've been mugging up that beastly drill, and can't remember a line of it.

CAPTAIN M. (*overhauling G.'s uniform*).—Go and tub. Don't bother me. I'll give you ten minutes to dress in.

Interval, filled by the noise as of a healthy grampus splashing in the bath-room.

CAPTAIN G. (*emerging from dressing-room*). What time is it?

CAPTAIN M.—Nearly eleven.

CAPTAIN G.—Five hours more. O Lord!

CAPTAIN M. (*aside*).—'First sign of funk, that. 'Wonder if it's going to spread. (*Aloud.*) Come along to breakfast.

CAPTAIN G.—I can't eat anything. I don't wan't any breakfast.

CAPTAIN. M. (*aside*).—So early! (*Aloud.*) Captain Gadsby, I *order* you to eat breakfast, and a dashed good breakfast, too. None of your bridal airs and graces with me!

Leads G. downstairs, and stands over him while he eats two chops.

CAPTAIN G. (*who has looked at his watch thrice in the last five minutes*).—What time is it?

CAPTAIN M.—Time to come for a walk. Light up.

CAPTAIN G.—I haven't smoked for ten days, and I won't now. (*Takes cheroot which M. has cut for him, and blows smoke through his nose luxuriously.*) We aren't going down the Mall, are we?

CAPTAIN M. (*aside*).—They're all alike in these stages. (*Aloud.*) No, my Vestal. We're going along the quietest road we can find.

CAPTAIN G.—Any chance of seeing Her?

CAPTAIN M.—Innocent! No! Come along, and, if you want me for the final obsequies, don't cut my eye out with your stick.

CAPTAIN G. (*spinning round*).—I say, isn't She the dearest creature that ever walked? What's the time? What comes after " wilt thou take this woman ? "

CAPTAIN M.—You go for the ring. R'clect it'll be on the top of my right-hand little finger, and just be careful how you draw it off, because I shall have the Verger's fees somewhere in my glove.

CAPTAIN G. (*walking forward hastily*).—D—— the Verger! Come along! It's past twelve, and I haven't seen Her since yesterday evening. (*Spinning round again.*) She's an absolute angel, Jack, and she's a dashed deal too good for me. Look here, does she come up the aisle on my arm, or how?

CAPTAIN M.—If I thought that there was the least chance of your remembering anything for two consecutive minutes, I'd tell you. Stop passaging about like that!

CAPTAIN G. (*halting in the middle of the road*).—I say, Jack.

CAPTAIN M.—Keep quiet for another ten minutes if you can, you lunatic, and *walk!*

The two tramp at five miles an hour for fifteen minutes.

CAPTAIN G.—What's the time? How about that cursed wedding-cake and the slippers? They don't throw 'em about in church, do they?

CAPTAIN M.—In-variably. The Padre leads off with his boots.

CAPTAIN G.—Confound your silly soul! Don't make fun of me. I can't stand it, and I won't!

CAPTAIN M. (*untroubled*).—So-ooo, old horse! You'll have to sleep for a couple of hours this afternoon.

CAPTAIN G. (*spinning round*).—I'm *not* going to be treated like a dashed child. Understand that!

CAPTAIN M. (*aside*).—Nerves gone to fiddlestrings. What a day we're having! (*Tenderly, putting his hand on G.'s shoulder.*) My David, how long have you known this Jonathan? Would I come up here to make a fool of you— after all these years?

CAPTAIN G. (*penitently*).—I know, I know, Jack—but I'm as upset as I can be. Don't mind what I say. Just hear me run through the drill and see if I've got it all right :—

" To have and to hold for better or worse, as it was in the beginning, is now, and ever shall be, world without end, so help me God.—Amen ".

CAPTAIN M. (*suffocating with suppressed laughter*).—Yes. That's about the gist of it. I'll prompt if you get into a hat.

CAPTAIN G. (*earnestly*).—Yes, you'll stick by me, Jack, won't you? I'm awf'ly happy, but I don't mind telling *you* that I'm in a blue funk!

CAPTAIN M. (*gravely*).—Are you? I should never have noticed it. You don't look as if you were.

CAPTAIN G.—Don't I? That's all right. (*Spinning round.*) On my soul and honour, Jack, She's the sweetest little angel that ever came down from the sky. There isn't a woman on earth fit to speak to Her!

CAPTAIN M. (*aside*).—And this is old Gaddy! (*Aloud.*) Go on if it relieves you.

CAPTAIN G.—You can laugh! That's all you wild asses of bachelors are fit for.

CAPTAIN M. (*drawling*).—You never would wait for the troop to come up. You aren't quite married yet, y'know.

CAPTAIN G.—Ugh! That reminds me. I don't believe I shall be able to get into my boots. Let's go home and try 'em on! (*Hurries forward.*)

CAPTAIN M.—'Wouldn't be in your shoes for anything that Asia has to offer.

CAPTAIN G. (*spinning round*).—That just shows your hideous blackness of soul—your dense stupidity—your brutal narrow-mindedness. There's only one fault about you. You're the best of good fellows, and I don't know what I should have done without you, but—you aren't married. (*Wags his head gravely.*) Take a wife, Jack.

CAPTAIN M. (*with a face like a wall*).—Ya-as. Whose for choice?

CAPTAIN G.—If you're going to be a blackguard I'm going on . . . What's the time?

CAPTAIN M. (*hums*):

"An' since 'twas very clear we drank only ginger beer,
Faith, there must ha' been some stingo in the ginger!"

Come back, you maniac. I'm going to take you home, and you're going to lie down.

CAPTAIN G.—What on earth do I want to lie down for?

CAPTAIN M.—Give me a light from your cheroot and see.

CAPTAIN G. (*watching cheroot-butt quiver like a tuning-fork*).—Sweet state I'm in!

CAPTAIN M.—You are. I'll get you a peg, and you'll go to sleep.

They return, and M. compounds a four-finger peg.

CAPTAIN G.—O, that's twice too much. It'll make me as drunk as an owl.

CAPTAIN M.—Curious thing, 'twon't have the slightest effect on you. Drink it off, chuck yourself down there, and go to bye-bye.

CAPTAIN G.—It's absurd. I shan't sleep. I *know* I shan't!

Falls into heavy doze at end of seven minutes. Captain M. watches him tenderly.

CAPTAIN M.—Poor old Gaddy! I've seen a few turned off before, but never one who went to the gallows in this condition. Can't tell how it affects 'em, though. It's the thorough-breds that sweat when they're backed into double-harness. . . . And that's the man who went through the guns at Amdheran like a devil possessed of devils. (*Leans over G.*) But this is worse than the guns, old pal—worse than the guns, isn't it? (*G. turns in his sleep, and M. touches him clumsily on the forehead.*) Poor, dear old Gaddy! Going like the rest of 'em—going like the rest of 'em. . . . Friend that sticketh closer than a brother. . . . eight years. Dashed bit of a slip of a girl. . . . eight weeks! And—where's your friend? (*Smokes disconsolately till Church clock strikes three.*)

CAPTAIN M.—Up with you! Get into your things.

CAPTAIN G.—Already? Isn't it too soon? Hadn't I better have a shave?

CAPTAIN M.—*No!* You're all right. (*Aside.*) He'd hack his chin to pieces.

CAPTAIN G.—What's the hurry ?

CAPTAIN M.—You've got to be there first.

CAPTAIN G.—To be stared at ?

CAPTAIN M.—Exactly. You're part of the show. Where's the burnisher ? Your spurs are in a shameful state.

CAPTAIN G. (*gruffly*).—Jack, I be damned if you shall do that for me.

CAPTAIN M. (*more gruffly*).—Dry up and get dressed ! If I choose to clean your spurs, you're under my orders.

Captain G. dresses, M. follows suit.

CAPTAIN M. (*critically, walking round*).—M'yes, you'll do. Only don't look so like a criminal. Ring, gloves, fees—that's all right for me. Let your moustache alone. Now, if the tats are ready, we'll go.

CAPTAIN G. (*nervously*).—It's much too soon. Let's light up ! Let's have a peg ! Let's ——

CAPTAIN M.—Let's make bally asses of ourselves.

BELLS (*without*).—*Good—peo—ple—all*
          To prayers—we call.

CAPTAIN M.—There go the bells ! Come on—unless you'd rather not. (*They ride off.*)

BELLS.—

> *We honour the King*
> *And Brides joy do bring—*
> *Good tidings we tell*
> *And ring the Dead's knell.*

CAPTAIN G. (*dismounting at the door of the Church*).—I say, aren't we much too soon ? There are no end of people inside. I say, aren't we much too late ? Stick by me Jack ! What the devil do I do ?

CAPTAIN M.—Strike an attitude at the head of the aisle and wait for Her. (*G. groans as M. wheels him into position before three hundred eyes.*)

CAPTAIN M. (*imploringly*).—Gaddy, if you love me, for pity's sake, for the Honour of the Regiment, stand up ! Chuck yourself into your uniform ! Look like a man ! I've got to speak to the Padre a minute. (*G. breaks into a gentle perspiration.*) If you wipe your face I'll *never* be your best man again. Stand *up!* (*G. trembles visibly.*)

CAPTAIN M. (*returning*).—She's coming now. Look out when the music starts. There's the organ beginning to clack.

Bride steps out of 'rickshaw at Church door. G. catches a glimpse of her and takes heart.

ORGAN (*Diapason and Burden*).—
> The Voice that breathed o'er Eden
> That earliest marriage day,
> The primal marriage blessing
> It hath not passed away.

CAPTAIN M. (*watching G.*).—By Jove! He *is* looking well. 'Didn't think he had it in him.

CAPTAIN G.—How long does this hymn go on for?

CAPTAIN M.—It will be over directly. (*Anxiously.*) Beginning to bleach and gulp? Hold on, Gaddy, and think o' the Regiment.

CAPTAIN G. (*measuredly*).—I say, there's a big brown lizard crawling up that wall.

CAPTAIN M.—My Sainted Mother! The last stage of collapse!

Bride comes up to left of altar, lifts her eyes once to G. who is suddenly smitten mad.

CAPTAIN G. (*to himself, again and again*).—Little Feather-weight's a woman—a woman! And I thought she was a little girl.

CAPTAIN M. (*in a whisper*).—From the halt—inward *wheel.*

Captain G. obeys mechanically, and the ceremony proceeds.

PADRE.—. . . only unto her as long as ye both shall live?

CAPTAIN G. (*his throat useless*).—Ha—hmmm!

CAPTAIN M.—Say you will or you won't. There's no second deal here.

Bride gives response with perfect coolness, and is given away by the father.

CAPTAIN G. (*thinking to show his learning*).—Jack, give me away now, *quick!*

CAPTAIN M.—You've given yourself away quite enough. Her *right* hand, man ! Repeat ! Repeat ! " Theodore Philip." Have you forgotten your own name ?

Captain G. stumbles through Affirmation which Bride repeats without a tremor.

CAPTAIN M.—Now the ring ! Follow the Padre ! Don't pull off my glove ! Here it is ! Great Cupid, he's found his voice !

G. repeats Troth in a voice to be heard to the end of the Church, and turns on his heel.

CAPTAIN M. (*desperately*).—Rein back ! Back to your troop ! 'Tisn't half legal yet.

PADRE.—. . . joined together, let no man put asunder.

Captain G., paralysed with fear, jibs after Blessing.

CAPTAIN M. (*quickly*).—On your own front—one length. Take her with you. I don't come. You've nothing to say. (*Captain G. jingles up to altar.*)

CAPTAIN M. (*in a piercing rattle, meant to be a whisper*).— Kneel, you stiff-necked ruffian ! Kneel !

PADRE.— . . . whose daughters ye are, so long as ye do well, and are not afraid with any amazement.

CAPTAIN M.—Dismiss ! Break off ! Left wheel !

All troop to vestry. They sign.

CAPTAIN M.—Kiss Her, Gaddy.

CAPTAIN G. (*rubbing ink-spot into his glove*).—Eh ! Wha—at ?

CAPTAIN M. (*taking one pace to Bride*).—If you don't, I shall.

CAPTAIN G. (*interposing an arm*).—Not this journey !

General kissing, in which Captain G. is pursued by un-known female.

CAPTAIN G. (*faintly to M.*)—This is Hades ! Can I wipe my face now ?

CAPTAIN M.—My responsibility has ended. Better ask *Missis* Gadsby.

Captain G. winces as if shot, and procession is Mendels-

sohned out of Church to paternal roof, where usual tortures take place over the wedding-cake.

CAPTAIN M. (*at table*).—Up with you, Gaddy.   They expect a speech.

CAPTAIN G. (*after three minutes' agony*).—Ha-hmmm! (*Thunders of applause.*)

CAPTAIN M.—Doocid good, for a first attempt.   Now go and change your kit while Mamma is weeping over—" the Missus ".   (*Captain G. disappears.   Captain M. starts up tearing his hair.*)   It's not *half* legal.   Where are the shoes? Get the ayah.

AYAH.—Missie Captain *Sahib* done gone hide away all the shoes.

CAPTAIN M. (*brandishing scabbarded sword*).—Woman, produce those shoes!   Some one lend me a bread-knife.   We mustn't crack Gaddy's head more than it is.   (*Slices heel off white satin slipper, and puts slipper up his sleeve.*)   Where is the Bride?   (*To the company at large.*)   Be tender with that rice.   It's a heathen custom.   Give me the big bag!

.   .   .   .

Bride slips out quietly into 'rickshaw and departs towards the sunset.

CAPTAIN M. (*in the open*).—Stole away, by Jove!   So much the worse for Gaddy!   Here he is.   Now, Gaddy, this'll be livelier than Amdheran!   Where's your horse?

CAPTAIN G. (*furiously, seeing that the women are out of earshot*).—Where the——is my *Wife*?

CAPTAIN M.—Half-way to Mahasu by this time.   You'll have to ride like Young Lochinvar.

Horse comes round on his hind legs; refuses to let G. handle him.

CAPTAIN G.—Oh, you will, will you?   Get round, you brute—you hog—you beast!   Get *round*.

Wrenches horse's head over, nearly breaking lower jaw; swings himself into saddle, and sends home both spurs in the midst of a spattering gale of Best Patna.

CAPTAIN M.—For your life and your love—ride, Gaddy!
—And God bless you!

*Throws half-a-pound of rice at G., who disappears, bowed
forward on the saddle, in a cloud of sunlit dust.*

CAPTAIN M.—I've lost old Gaddy.   (*Lights cigarette and
strolls off, singing absently*) :—

You may carve it on his tombstone, you may cut it on
   his card,

That a young man married is a young man marred!

MISS DEERCOURT (*from her horse*).—Really, Captain
Mafflin!   You are more plainspoken than polite!

CAPTAIN M. (*aside*).—They say marriage is like cholera.
Wonder who'll be the next victim.

*White satin slipper slides from his sleeve and falls at his
feet.   Left wondering.*

CURTAIN.

THE GARDEN OF EDEN.

" And ye shall be as—Gods ? "

SCENE.—*Thymy grass-plot at back of the Mahasu rest-house, overlooking little wooded valley. On the left, glimpse of the Dead Forest of Fagoo ; on the right, Simla Hills. In background, line of the Snows. Captain Gadsby, now one week a husband, is smoking the pipe of peace on a rug in the sunshine. Banjo and tobacco-pouch on rug. Overhead, the Fagoo eagles. Mrs. G. comes out of the house.*

MRS G.—My husband !

CAPTAIN G. (*lazily, with intense enjoyment*).—Eh, wha-at ? Say that again.

MRS G.—I've written to Mamma and told her that we shall be back on the seventeenth.

CAPTAIN G.—Did you give her my love ?

MRS. G.—No, I kept all that for myself. (*Sitting down by his side.*) I thought you wouldn't mind.

CAPTAIN G. (*with mock sternness*).—I object awf'ly. How did you know that it was yours to keep ?

MRS. G.—I guessed, Phil.

CAPTAIN G. (*rapturously*).—*Lit-tle* Featherweight !

MRS. G.—I won't be called those sporting pet names, bad boy.

CAPTAIN G.—You'll be called anything I choose. Has it ever occurred to you, Madam, that you are my Wife ?

Mrs. G.—It has. I haven't ceased wondering at it yet.

CAPTAIN G.—Nor I. It seems so strange ; and yet, somehow, it doesn't. (*Confidently.*) You see, it could have been no one else.

MRS. G. (*softly*).—No. No one else—for me or for you. It must have been all arranged from the beginning. Phil, tell me again what made you care for me.

CAPTAIN G.—How could I help it? You were *you*, you know.

MRS. G.—Did you ever want to help it? Speak the truth?

CAPTAIN G. (*a twinkle in his eye*).—I did, darling, just at the first. But only at the very first. (*Chuckles.*) I called you—stoop low and I'll whisper—" a little beast ". Ho! Ho! Ho!

MRS. G. (*taking him by the moustache and making him sit up*).—" A—little—beast ! " Stop laughing over your crime ! And yet you had the—the—awful cheek to propose to me !

CAPTAIN G.—I'd changed my mind then. And you weren't a little beast any more.

MRS. G.—Thank you, Sir ! And when was I ever ?

CAPTAIN G.—Never ! But that first day, when you gave me tea in that peach-coloured muslin gown thing, you looked—you did, indeed, dear—such an absurd little mite. And I didn't know what to say to you.

MRS. G. (*twisting moustache*).—So you said " little beast ". Upon my word, Sir ! *I* called *you* a " Crrrreature," but I wish now I had called you something worse.

CAPTAIN G. (*very meekly*).—I apologize, but you're hurting me awf'ly. (*Interlude.*) You're welcome to torture me again on those terms.

MRS. G.—Oh, *why* did you let me do it?

CAPTAIN G. (*looking across valley*).—No reason in particular, but—if it amused you or did you any good—you might— wipe those dear little boots of yours on me.

MRS. G. (*stretching out her hands*).—Don't ! Oh don't ! Philip, my King, *please* don't talk like that. It's how *I* feel. You're so much too good for me. So much too good !

CAPTAIN G.—Me ! I'm not fit to put my arm round you. (*Puts it round.*)

MRS. G.—Yes, you are. But I—what have I ever done?

CAPTAIN G.—Given me a wee bit of your heart, haven't you, my Queen ?

MRS. G.—That's nothing.   Any one would do that,
They cou—couldn't help it.

CAPTAIN G.—Pussy, you'll make me horribly conceited.
Just when I was beginning to feel so humble, too.

MRS. G.—Humble !   I don't believe it's in your character.

CAPTAIN G.—What do you know of my character, Imperti-
nence ?

MRS. G.—Ah, but I shall, shan't I, Phil ?   I shall have
time, in all the years and years to come, to know everything
about you ; and there will be no secrets between us.

CAPTAIN G.—Little witch !   I believe you know me
thoroughly already.

MRS. G.—I think I can guess.   You're selfish ?

CAPTAIN G.—Yes.

MRS. G.—Foolish ?

CAPTAIN G.—Very.

MRS. G.—And a dear ?

CAPTAIN G.—That is as my lady pleases.

MRS. G.—Then your lady *is* pleased.   (*A pause.*)   D'you
know that we're two, solemn, serious, grown-up people——

CAPTAIN G. (*tilting her straw hat over her eyes*).—You
grown up !   Pooh !   You're a baby.

MRS. G.—And we're talking nonsense.

CAPTAIN G.—Then let's go on talking nonsense.   I rather
like it.   Pussy, I'll tell you a secret.   Promise not to repeat ?

MRS. G.—Ye—es.   Only to you.

CAPTAIN G.—I love you.

MRS. G.—Re-ally ?   For how long ?

CAPTAIN G.—For ever and ever.

MRS. G.—That's a long time.

CAPTAIN G.—'Think so ?   It's the shortest I can do with.

MRS. G.—You're getting quite clever.

CAPTAIN G.—I'm talking to *you.*

MRS. G.—Prettily turned.   Hold up your stupid old
head, and I'll pay you for it !

CAPTAIN G. (*affecting supreme contempt*).—Take it yourself
if you want it.

MRS. G.—I've a great mind to. . . . and I will! (*Takes it, and is repaid with interest.*)

CAPTAIN G.—Little Featherweight, it's my opinion that we *are* a couple of idiots.

MRS. G.—We're the only two sensible people in the world! Ask the eagle. He's coming by.

CAPTAIN G.—Ah! I dare say he's seen a good many sensible people at Mahasu. They say that those birds live for ever so long.

MRS. G.—How long?

CAPTAIN G.—A hundred and twenty years.

MRS. G.—A hundred and twenty years! O-oh! And in a hundred and twenty years where will these two sensible people be?

CAPTAIN G.—What does it matter so long as we are together now?

MRS. G. (*looking round the horizon*).—Yes. Only you and I—I and you—in the whole wide, wide world until the end. (*Sees the line of the Snows.*) How big and quiet the hills look! D'you think they care for us?

CAPTAIN G.—Can't say I've consulted 'em particularly. *I* care, and that's enough for me.

MRS. G. (*drawing nearer to him*).—Yes, now. . . . but afterwards. What's that little black blur on the Snows?

CAPTAIN G.—A snowstorm, forty miles away. You'll see it move, as the wind carries it across the face of that spur, and then it will be all gone.

MRS. G.—And then it will be all gone. (*Shivers.*)

CAPTAIN G. (*anxiously*).—'Not chilled, pet, are you? 'Better let me get your cloak.

MRS. G.—No. Don't leave me, Phil. Stay here. I believe I'm afraid. Oh, why are the hills so *horrid?* Phil, promise me, promise me that you'll always, *always* love me.

CAPTAIN G.—What's the trouble, darling? I can't promise any more than I have; but I'll promise that again and again if you like.

MRS. G. (*her head on his shoulder*).—Say it, then—say it!

N-no—don't! The—the—eagles would laugh. (*Recovering.*) My husband, you've married a little goose.

CAPTAIN G. (*very tenderly*).—Have I? I am content whatever she is, so long as she is mine.

MRS. G. (*quickly*).—Because she is yours, or because she is me mineself?

CAPTAIN G.—Because she is both. (*Piteously.*) I'm not clever, dear, and I don't think I can make myself understood properly.

MRS. G.—*I* understand. Pip, will you tell me something?

CAPTAIN G.—Anything you like. (*Aside.*) I wonder what's coming now.

MRS. G. (*haltingly, her eyes lowered*).—You told me once in the old days—centuries and centuries ago—that you had been engaged before. I didn't say anything—then.

CAPTAIN G. (*innocently*).—Why not?

MRS. G. (*raising her eyes to his*).—Because—because I was afraid of losing you, my heart. But now—tell about it—*please.*

CAPTAIN G.—There's nothing to tell. I was awf'ly old then—nearly two and twenty—and she was quite that.

MRS. G.—That means she was older than you. I shouldn't like her to have been younger. Well?

CAPTAIN G.—Well, I fancied myself in love and raved about a bit, and—Oh, yes, by Jove! I made up poetry. Ha! ha!

MRS. G.—You never wrote any for *me!* What happened?

CAPTAIN G.—I came out here, and the whole thing went to pieces. She wrote to say that there had been a mistake, and then she married.

MRS. G.—Did she care for you much?

CAPTAIN G.—No. At least she didn't show it as far as I remember.

MRS. G.—As far as you remember! Do you remember her name? (*Hears it, and bows her head.*) Thank you, my husband.

CAPTAIN G.—Who but you had the right? Now, Little Featherweight, have you ever been mixed up in any dark and dismal tragedy?

MRS. G.—If you call me Mrs. Gadsby, p'raps I'll tell.

CAPTAIN G. (*throwing parade rasp into his voice*).—Mrs. Gadsby confess!

MRS. G.—Good Heavens, Phil! I never knew that you could speak in that terrible voice.

CAPTAIN G.—You don't know half my accomplishments yet. Wait till we are settled in the plains and I'll show you how I bark at my troop. You were going to say, darling?

MRS. G.—I—I don't like to, after that voice. (*Tremulously.*) Phil, never you *dare* to speak to me in that tone, whatever I may do!

CAPTAIN G.—My poor, little love! Why, you're shaking all over! I *am* so sorry! Of course I never meant to upset you. Don't tell me anything. I'm a brute.

MRS. G.—No, you aren't, and I *will* tell. . . . There was a man.

CAPTAIN G. (*lightly*).—Was there? Lucky man!

MRS. G. (*in a whisper*).—And I thought I cared for him.

CAPTAIN G.—Still luckier man! Well?

MRS. G.—And I thought I cared for him—and I didn't— and then you came—and I cared for you very, *very* much indeed. That's all. (*Face hidden.*) You aren't angry, are you?

CAPTAIN G.—Angry? Not in the least. (*Aside.*) Good Lord, what have I done to deserve this angel?

MRS. G. (*aside*).—And he never asked for the name! How funny men are! But perhaps it's as well.

CAPTAIN G.—That man will go to Heaven because you once thought you cared for him. 'Wonder if you'll ever drag me up there?

MRS. G. (*firmly*).—'Shan't go if you don't.

CAPTAIN G.—Thanks. I say, Pussy, I don't know much about your religious beliefs. You were brought up to believe in a Heaven and all that, weren't you?

MRS. G.—Yes. But it was a pincushion Heaven with hymn-books in all the pews.

CAPTAIN G. (*wagging his head with intense conviction*).— Never mind. There is a real Heaven.

MRS. G.—Where do you bring that message from, my prophet?

CAPTAIN G.—Here! Because we care for each other. So it's all right.

MRS. G. (*as a troop of grey monkeys crash through the branches*).—So it's all right. But Darwin says that we came from *those*!

CAPTAIN G. (*placidly*).—Ah! Darwin was never in love with an angel. That settles it. Sstt, you brutes! Monkeys, indeed! You shouldn't read those books.

MRS. G. (*folding her hands*).—If it pleaseth my Lord the King to issue proclamation ——

CAPTAIN G.— Don't, dear one. There are no orders between us. Only I'd rather you didn't. They lead to nothing and bother people's heads.

MRS. G.—Like your first engagement?

CAPTAIN G. (*with an immense calm*).—That was a necessary evil and led to you. Are you nothing?

MRS. G.—Not so very much, am I?

CAPTAIN G.—All this world and the next to me.

MRS. G. (*very softly*).—My boy of boys! Shall I tell *you* something?

CAPTAIN G.—Yes, if it's not dreadful—about other men.

MRS. G.—It's about my own, bad, little self.

CAPTAIN G.—Then it must be good. Go on, dear.

MRS. G. (*slowly*).—I don't know why I'm telling you Pip; but if ever you marry again—(*interlude*). Take your hand from my mouth or I'll *bite*! In the future, then remember . . . I don't know quite how to put it!

CAPTAIN G. (*snorting indignantly*).—Don't try. "Marry again" indeed!

MRS. G—I must. Listen, my husband. Never, never,

never tell your wife anything that you do not wish her to remember and think over all her life. Because a woman— yes, I am a woman, sir—*can't* forget.

CAPTAIN G.—By Jove, how do *you* know that?

MRS. G. (*confusedly*).—I don't. I'm only guessing. I am—I was—a silly, little girl; but I feel that I know so much, oh, so very much more than you, dearest. To begin with, I'm your wife.

CAPTAIN G.—So I have been led to believe.

MRS. G.—And I shall want to know every one of your secrets—to share everything you know with you. (*Stares round desperately for lucidity and coherence.*)

CAPTAIN G.—So you shall, dear—so you shall; but don't look like that.

MRS. G.—For your own sake don't stop me, Phil. I shall never talk to you in this way again. You must *not* tell me! At least, not now. Later on, when I'm an old matron it won't matter, but if you love me, be very good to me now; for this part of my life I shall *never* forget! Have I made you understand?

CAPTAIN G.—I think so, child. Have I said anything yet that you disapprove of?

MRS. G.—Will you be very angry? That—that voice and what you said about the engagement ——

CAPTAIN G.—But you asked to be told that, darling.

MRS. G.—And *that's* why you shouldn't have told me! You must be the judge; and, O Pip! dearly as I love you, I shan't be able to help you! I shall hinder you, and you must judge in spite of me!

CAPTAIN G. (*meditatively*).—We have a great many things to find out together, God help us both—say so, Pussy—but we shall understand each other better every day; and I think I'm beginning to see now. How in the world did you come to know just the importance of giving me just that lead?

MRS. G.—I've told you that I don't know. Only somehow it seemed that, in all this new life, I was being guided for your sake as well as my own.

CAPTAIN G. (*aside*).—Then Mafflin was right! They know, and we—we're blind—all of us. (*Lightly.*) 'Getting a little beyond our depth, dear, aren't we? I'll remember, and, if I fail, let me be punished as I deserve.

MRS. G.—There shall be no punishment. We'll start into life together from here—you and I—and no one else.

CAPTAIN G.—And no one else. (*A pause.*) Your eyelashes are all wet, Sweet? Was there ever such a quaint, little Absurdity?

MRS. G.—Was there ever such nonsense talked before?

CAPTAIN G. (*knocking the ashes out of his pipe*).—'Tisn't what we say, it's what we don't say that helps. And it's all the profoundest philosophy. But no one would understand—even if it were put into a book.

MRS. G.—The idea! No—only we ourselves, or people like ourselves—if there are any people like us.

CAPTAIN G. (*magisterially*).—All people not like ourselves are blind idiots.

MRS. G. (*wiping her eyes*).—Do you think, then, that there are any people as happy as we are?

CAPTAIN G.—'Must be—unless we've appropriated all the happiness in the world.

MRS. G. (*looking towards Simla*).—Poor dears! Just fancy, if we have!

CAPTAIN G.—Then we'll hang on to the whole show, for it's a great deal too jolly to lose—eh, wife o' mine?

MRS. G.—Oh, Pip, Pip! How much of you is a solemn married man, and how much a horrid, slangy schoolboy?

CAPTAIN G.—When you tell me how much of you was eighteen last birthday, and how much is as old as the Sphinx and twice as mysterious, perhaps I'll attend to you. Lend me that banjo. The spirit moveth me to yowl at the sunset.

MRS. G.—Mind! It's not tuned. Ah! How that jars!

CAPTAIN G. (*turning pegs*).—It's amazingly difficult to keep a banjo to proper pitch.

MRS. G.—It's the same with all musical instruments. What shall it be?

CAPTAIN G.—" *Vanity,*" and let the hills hear. (*Sings through the first and half of the second verse. Turning to Mrs. G.*) Now, chorus! Sing, Pussy

BOTH TOGETHER (*con brio, to the horror of the monkeys, who are settling for the night*).

"Vanity, all is Vanity," said Wisdom, scorning me—
I clasped my true Love's tender hand, and answered
    frank and free—ee :—
" If this be Vanity, who'd be wise?
" If this be Vanity, who'd be wise?
" If this be Vanity, who'd be wi—ise?
(*Crescendo.*)—" Vanity let it be!"

MRS. G. (*defiantly, to the grey of the evening sky*).—" Vanity let it be!"

ECHO (*from the Fagoo spur*).—Let it be!

CURTAIN.

FATIMA.

" And you may go into every room of the house and see everything that is there, but into the Blue Room you must not go."—The Story of Blue Beard.

SCENE.—*The Gadsby's bungalow in the Plains. Time, 11 a.m. on a Sunday morning. Captain Gadsby, in his shirt-sleeves, is bending over a complete set of hussar's equipment from saddle to picketing-rope, which is neatly spread over the floor of his study. He is smoking an unclean briar, and his forehead is puckered with thought.*

CAPTAIN G. (*to himself, fingering a headstall*).—Jack's an ass! There's enough brass on this to load a mule . . . and, if the Americans know anything about anything, it can be cut down to a bit only. 'Don't want the watering-bridle either. Humbug! . . . Half-a-dozen sets of chains and pulleys for the same old horse! (*Scratching his head.*) Now, let's consider it all over from the beginning. By Jove, I've forgotten the scale of weights! Ne'er mind. 'Keep the bit only, and eliminate every boss from the crupper to the breast-plate. No breastplate at all. Simple leather strap across the breast—like the Russians. Hi! Jack never thought of *that!*

MRS. G. (*entering hastily, her hand bound in a cloth*).—Oh, Pip! I've scalded my hand over that horrid, horrid Tiparee jam.

CAPTAIN G. (*absently*).—Eh! Wha-at?

MRS. G. (*with round-eyed reproach*).—I've scalded it *aw*-fully! Aren't you sorry? And I did so want that jam to jam properly.

CAPTAIN G.—Poor little woman! Let me kiss the place and make it well. (*Unrolling bandage.*) You small sinner! Where's that scald? I can't see it.

MRS. G.—On the top of the little finger. There!—It's a most 'normous big burn!

CAPTAIN G. (*kissing little finger*).—Baby ! Let Hyder look after the jam. You know I don't care for sweets.

MRS. G.—In-deed ? . . . Pip !

CAPTAIN G.—Not of that kind, anyhow. And now run along, Minnie, and leave me to my own base devices. I'm busy.

MRS. G. (*calmly, settling herself in long chair*).—So I see. What a mess you're making ! Why have you brought all that smelly leather stuff into the house ?

CAPTAIN G.—To play with. Do you mind, dear ?

MRS. G.—Let me play too. I'd like it.

CAPTAIN G.—I'm afraid you wouldn't, Pussy . . . Don't you think that jam will burn, or whatever it is that jam does when it's not looked after by a clever little housekeeper ?

MRS. G.—I thought you said Hyder could attend to it. I left him in the verandah, stirring—when I hurt myself so.

CAPTAIN G. (*his eye returning to the equipment*).—Po-oor little woman ! . . . Three pound four and seven is three eleven, and that can be cut down to two eight with just a *lee*-tle care, without weakening anything. Farriery is all rot in incompetent hands. What's the use of a shoecase when a man's scouting ? He can't stick it on with a lick—like a stamp—the shoe ! Skittles !

MRS. G.—What's skittles ! Pah ! What *is* this leather cleaned with ?

CAPTAIN G.—Cream and champagne and . . . Look here, dear, do you really want to talk to me about anything important ?

MRS. G.—No. I've done my accounts, and I thought I'd like to see what you're doing.

CAPTAIN G.—Well, love, now you've seen and . . . Would you mind ? . . . That is to say . . . Minnie, I really am busy.

MRS. G.—You want me to go ?

CAPTAIN G.—Yes, dear, for a little while. This tobacco will hang in your dress, and saddlery doesn't interest you.

MRS. G.—Everything you do interests me, Pip.

CAPTAIN G.—Yes, I know, I know, dear. I'll tell you all about it some day, when I've put a head on this thing. In the meantime ——

MRS. G.—I'm to be turned out of the room like a trouble-some child?

CAPTAIN G.—No-o. I don't mean that exactly. But, you see, I shall be tramping up and down, shifting these things to and fro, and I shall be in your way? Don't you think so?

MRS. G.—Can't I lift them about? Let me try (*reaches forward to trooper's saddle*).

CAPTAIN G.—Good gracious, child, don't touch it. You'll hurt yourself (*picking up saddle*). Little girls aren't expected to handle accoutrements. Now, where would you like it put? (*Holds saddle above his head.*)

MRS. G. (*a break in her voice*).—Nowhere. Pip, how good you are—and how strong! Oh, what's that ugly red streak inside your arm?

CAPTAIN G. (*lowering saddle quickly*).—Nothing. It's a mark of sorts. (*Aside.*) And Jack's coming to tiffin, with his notions all cut and dried!

MRS. G.—I know it's a mark, but I've never seen it before. It runs all up the arm. What is it?

CAPTAIN G.—A cut—if you want to know!

MRS. G.—Want to know! Of course I do! I can't have my husband cut to pieces in this way. How did it come? Was it an accident? Tell me, Pip.

CAPTAIN G. (*grimly*).—No; 'twasn't an accident. I got it—from a man—in Afghanistan.

MRS. G.—In action? O Pip, and you *never* told me!

CAPTAIN G.—I'd forgotten all about it.

MRS. G.—Hold up your arm! What a horrid, ugly scar! Are you sure it doesn't hurt now? How did the man give it you?

CAPTAIN G. (*desperately, looking at his watch*).—With a

knife. I came down—old *Van Loo* did, that's to say—and
fell on my leg, so I couldn't run. And then this man came
up, and began chopping at me as I sprawled.

MRS. G.—Oh, don't, don't! That's enough!... Well,
what happened?

CAPTAIN G.—I couldn't get to my holster, and Mafflin
came round the corner and stopped the performance.

MRS. G.—How? He's such a lazy man. I don't believe
he did.

CAPTAIN G.—Don't you? I don't think the man had
much doubt about it. Jack cut his head off.

MRS. G.—Cut—his—head—off! "With one blow," as
they say in the books?

CAPTAIN G.—I'm not sure. I was too interested in myself to know much about it. Anyhow the head was off, and
Jack was punching old *Van Loo* in the ribs to make him get
up. Now, you know all about it, dear, and now ——

MRS. G.—You want me to go, of course. You never told
me about this, though I've been married to you for *ever* so
long; and you never *would* have told me if I hadn't found
out; and you never *do* tell me anything about yourself, or
what you do, or what you take an interest in.

CAPTAIN G.—Darling, I'm always with you, aren't I?

MRS. G.—Always in my pocket, you were going to say.
I know you are; but you are always *thinking* away from me.

CAPTAIN G. (*trying to hide a smile*).—Am I? I wasn't
aware of it. I'm awf'ly sorry.

MRS. G. (*piteously*).—Oh, don't make fun of me! Pip,
you know what I mean. When you are reading one of those
things about cavalry, by that idiotic Prince—why doesn't he
be a Prince, instead of a stable-boy?

CAPTAIN G.—Prince Kraft a stable-boy! Oh, my Aunt!
Never mind, dear! You were going to say?

MRS. G.—It doesn't matter. You don't care for what I
say. Only—only you get up and walk about the room,
staring in front of you, and then Mafflin comes in to dinner,

and after I'm in the drawing-room I can hear you and him talking and talking and talking about things I can't understand, and—O I get *so* tired and feel *so* lonely!—I don't want to complain and be a trouble, Pip; but I do—indeed I do!

CAPTAIN G.—My poor darling! I never thought of that, Why don't you ask some nice people in to dinner?

MRS. G.—Nice people! Where am I to find them? Horrid frumps! And if I did, I shouldn't be amused. You know I only want you.

CAPTAIN G.—And you have me surely, Sweetheart?

MRS. G.—I have not! Pip, why don't you take me into your life?

CAPTAIN G.—More than I do? That would be difficult dear.

MRS. G.—Yes, I suppose it would—to you. I'm no help to you—no companion to you; and you like to have it so.

CAPTAIN G.—Aren't you a little unreasonable, Pussy?

MRS. G. (*stamping her foot*).—I'm the most reasonable woman in the world—when I'm treated properly.

CAPTAIN G.—And since when have I been treating you improperly?

MRS. G.—Always—and since the beginning. You *know* you have.

CAPTAIN G.—I don't. But I'm willing to be convinced.

MRS. G. (*pointing to saddlery*).—There!

CAPTAIN G.—How do you mean?

MRS. G.—What does all that mean? Why am I not to be told? Is it so precious?

CAPTAIN G.—I forget its exact Government value just at present. It means that it is a great deal too heavy.

MRS. G.—Then why do you touch it?

CAPTAIN G.—To make it lighter. See here, little love, I've one notion and Jack has another, but we are both agreed that all this equipment is about thirty pounds too heavy. The thing is how to cut it down without weakening any part of it, and, at the same time, allowing the trooper to carry everything he wants for his own comfort—socks and shirts and things of that kind.

MRS. G.—Why doesn't he pack them in a little trunk?

CAPTAIN G. (*kissing her*).—Oh, you darling! Pack them in a little trunk, indeed! Hussars don't carry trunks, and it's a most important thing to make the horse do all the carrying.

MRS. G.—But why need *you* bother about it? You're not a trooper.

CAPTAIN G.—No; but I command a few score of him, and equipment is nearly everything in these days.

MRS. G.—More than *me?*

CAPTAIN G.—Stupid! Of course not; but it's a matter that I'm tremendously interested in, because if I or Jack, or I and Jack, hack out some sort of lighter saddlery and all that, it's possible that we may get it adopted.

MRS. G.—How?

CAPTAIN G.—Sanctioned at Home, where they will make a sealed pattern—a pattern that all the saddlers must copy—and so it will be used by all the regiments.

MRS. G.—And that interests you?

CAPTAIN G.—It's part of my profession, y'know, and my profession is a good deal to me. Everything in a soldier's equipment is important, and if we can improve that equipment so much the better for the soldiers and for us.

MRS. G.—Who's "us?"

CAPTAIN G.—Jack and I; though Jack's notions are too radical. What's that big sigh for, Minnie?

MRS. G.—Oh, nothing—and you've kept all this a secret from me? Why?

CAPTAIN G.—Not a secret exactly, dear. I didn't say anything about it to you because I didn't think it would amuse you.

MRS. G.—And am I only made to be amused?

CAPTAIN G.—No, of course. I merely mean that it couldn't interest you.

5

Mrs. G.—It's *your* work and—and, if you'd let me, I'd count all these things up. If they are too heavy, you know by how much they are too heavy, and you must have a list of things made out to your scale of lightness, and ——

Captain G.—I've got both scales somewhere in my head; but it's hard to tell how light you can make a head-stall, for instance, until you have actually had a model made.

Mrs. G.—But if you read out the list, I could copy it down, and pin it up there just above your table. Wouldn't that do ?

Captain G.—It would be awf'ly nice, dear, but it would be giving you trouble for nothing. I can't work that way. I go by rule of thumb. I know the present scale of weights, and the other one—the one that I'm trying to work to—will shift and vary so much that I couldn't be certain, even if I wrote it down.

Mrs. G.—I'm *so* sorry. I thought I might help. Is there anything else that I could be of use in ?

Captain G. (*looking round the room*).—I can't think of anything. You're *always* helping me, you know.

Mrs. G.—Am I ? How ?

Captain G.—You are you of course, and as long as you're near me—I can't explain exactly, but it's in the air.

Mrs. G.—And that's why you wanted to send me away?

Captain G.—That's only when I'm trying to do work— grubby work like this.

Mrs. G.—Mafflin's better then, isn't he ?

Captain G. (*rashly*).—Of course he is. Jack and I have been thinking down the same grove for two or three years, about this equipment. It's our hobby, and it may really be useful some day.

Mrs. G. (*after a pause*).—And that's all that you have away from me ?

Captain G.—It isn't very far away from you now. Take care that the oil on that bit doesn't come off on your dress.

Mrs. G.—I wish—I wish so much that I could really

help you. I believe I could—if I left the room. But that's not what I mean.

CAPTAIN G. (*aside*).—Give me patience! I wish she would go. (*Aloud.*) I assure you you can't do anything for me, Minnie, and I must really settle down to this. Where's my pouch?

MRS. G. (*crossing to writing-table*).—Here you are, Bear. What a mess you keep your table in!

CAPTAIN G.—Don't touch it. There's a method in my madness, though you mightn't think it.

MRS. G. (*at table*).—I want to look—Do you keep accounts, Pip?

CAPTAIN G. (*bending over saddlery*).—Of a sort. Are you rummaging among the Troop papers? Be careful.

MRS. G.—Why? I shan't disturb anything. Good gracious! I had no idea that you had anything to do with so many sick horses.

CAPTAIN G.—'Wish I hadn't, but they insist on falling sick. Minnie, if I were you, I really should not investigate those papers. You may come across something that you won't like.

MRS. G.—Why will you always treat me like a child? I know I'm not displacing the horrid things.

CAPTAIN G. (*resignedly*).—Very well, then. Don't blame me if anything happens. Play with the table and let me go on with the saddlery. (*Slipping hand into trouser-pocket.*) Oh, the deuce!

MRS. G. (*her back to G.*).—What's that for?

CAPTAIN G.—Nothing. (*Aside.*) There's not much of importance in it, but I wish I'd torn it up.

MRS. G. (*turning over contents of table*).—I know you'll hate me for this; but I want to see what your work is like. (*A pause.*) Pip, what are "farcy-buds"?

CAPTAIN G.—Hah! Would you really like to know? They aren't pretty things.

MRS. G.—This Journal of Veterinary Science says they are of "absorbing interest". Tell me.

CAPTAIN G. (*aside*).—It may turn her attention.

Gives a long and designedly loathsome account of glanders and farcy.

MRS. G.—Oh, that's enough. Don't go on!

CAPTAIN G.—But you wanted to know. Then these things suppurate and matterate and spread ——

MRS. G.—Pip, you're making me sick! You're a horrid, disgusting school-boy.

CAPTAIN G. (*on his knees among the bridles*).—You asked to be told. It's not my fault if you worry me into talking about horrors.

MRS. G.—Why didn't you say no?

CAPTAIN G.—Good Heavens, child! Have you come in here simply to bully me?

MRS. G.—I bully *you?* How could I! You're so strong. (*Hysterically.*) Strong enough to pick me up and put me outside the door, and leave me there to cry. Aren't you?

CAPTAIN G.—It seems to me that you're an irrational little baby. Are you quite well?

MRS. G.—Do I look ill? (*Returning to table.*) Who is your lady friend with the big grey envelope and the fat monogram outside?

CAPTAIN G. (*aside*).—Then it wasn't in the drawers, confound it. (*Aloud.*) "God made her, therefore let her pass for a woman." You remember what farcy-buds are like?

MRS. G. (*showing envelope*).—This has nothing to do with *them*. I'm going to open it. May I?

CAPTAIN G.—Certainly, if you want to. I'd sooner you didn't though. I don't ask to look at your letters to the Deercourt girl.

MRS. G.—You'd *better* not, Sir! (*Takes letter from envelope.*) Now may I look? If you say no, I shall cry.

CAPTAIN G.—You've never cried in my knowledge of you, and I don't believe you could.

MRS. G.—I feel very like it to-day, Pip. Don't be hard on me. (*Reads letter.*) It begins in the middle, without any "Dear Captain Gadsby" or anything. How funny!

CAPTAIN G. (*aside*).—No, it's not Dear Captain Gadsby or anything, now. How funny!

MRS. G.—What a strange letter! (*Reads.*) " And so the moth has come too near the candle at last, and has been singed into—shall I say Respectability? I congratulate him, and hope he will be as happy as he deserves to be." What does that mean? Is she congratulating you about our marriage?

CAPTAIN G.—Yes, I suppose so.

MRS. G. (*still reading letter*).—She seems to be a particular friend of yours.

CAPTAIN G.—Yes. She was an excellent matron of sorts —a Mrs. Herriott—wife of a Colonel Herriott. I used to know some of her people at home long ago—before I came out.

MRS. G.—Some Colonel's wives are young—as young as me. I knew one who was younger.

CAPTAIN G.—Then it couldn't have been Mrs. Herriott. She was old enough to have been your mother, dear.

MRS. G.—I remember now. Mrs. Scargill was talking about her at the Duffius' tennis, before you came for me, on Tuesday. Captain Mafflin said she was a " dear old woman ". Do you know I think Mafflin is a very clumsy man with his feet.

CAPTAIN G. (*aside*).—Good old Jack! (*Aloud.*) Why, dear.

MRS. G.—He had put his cup down on the ground then, and he literally stepped into it. Some of the tea spirted over my dress—the grey one. I meant to tell you about it before.

CAPTAIN G. (*aside*).—There are the makings of a strategist about Jack, though his methods are coarse. (*Aloud.*) You'd better get a new dress, then. (*Aside.*) Let us pray that that will turn her.

MRS. G.—Oh, it isn't stained in the least. I only thought that I'd tell you. (*Returning to letter.*) *What* an extra-

ordinary person! (*Reads.*) " But need I remind you that you
have taken upon yourself a charge of wardship "—what in the
world is a charge of wardship?—" which, as you yourself
know, may end in Consequences ——"

CAPTAIN G. (*aside*).—It's safest to let 'em see everything
as they come across it: but 'seems to me that there are ex-
ceptions to the rule. (*Aloud.*) I told you that there was
nothing to be gained from re-arranging my table.

MRS. G. (*absently*).—What *does* the woman mean? She
goes on talking about Consequences—" almost inevitable Consequences " with a capital C—for half a page. (*Flushing
scarlet.*) Oh, good gracious! How abominable!

CAPTAIN G. (*promptly*). Do you think so? Doesn't it
show a sort of motherly interest in us? (*Aside.*) Thank
Heaven, Harry always wrapped her meaning up safely.
(*Aloud.*) *Is* it absolutely necessary to go on with the letter,
darling?

MRS. G.—It's impertinent—it's simply horrid. What
right has this woman to write in this way to you? She
oughtn't to.

CAPTAIN G.—When you write to the Deercourt girl I
notice that you generally fill three or four sheets. Can't you
let an old woman babble on paper once in a way? She
means well.

MRS. G.—I don't care. She shouldn't write, and if she
did, you ought to have shown me her letter.

CAPTAIN G.—Can't you understand why I kept it to
myself, or must I explain at length—as I explained the
farcy-buds?

MRS. G. (*furiously*).—Pip, I *hate* you! This is as bad as
those idiotic saddle-bags on the floor. Never mind whether
it would please me or not, you ought to have given it to me
to read.

CAPTAIN G.—It comes to the same thing. You took it
yourself.

MRS. G.—Yes, but if I hadn't taken it, you wouldn't have

said a word. I think this Harriet Herriott—it's like a name
in a book—is an interfering old Thing.

CAPTAIN G. (*aside*).—So long as you thoroughly understand that she *is* old, I don't much care what you think.
(*Aloud.*) Very good, dear. Would you like to write and tell
her so ? She's seven thousand miles away.

MRS. G.—I don't want to have anything to do with her;
but you ought to have told me. (*Turning to last page of
letter.*) And she patronizes me, too. *I*'ve never seen her !
(*Reads.*) "I do not know how the world stands with you.
In all human probability I shall never know, but whatever I
may have said before, I pray for *her* sake more than for yours
that all may be well. I have learnt what misery means, and
I dare not wish that anyone dear to you should share my
knowledge."

CAPTAIN G.—Good God ! Can't you leave that letter
alone, or, at least, can't you refrain from reading it aloud ?
I've been through it once. Put it back on the desk. Do
you hear me ?

MRS. G. (*irresolutely*).—I sh—shan't ! (*Looks at G.'s eyes.*)
Oh, Pip, *please !* I didn't mean to make you angry—'Deed,
I didn't. Pip, I'm so sorry. I know I've wasted your
time ——

CAPTAIN G. (*grimly*).—You have. Now, will you be good
enough to go—if there is nothing more in my room that
you are anxious to pry into ?

MRS. G. (*putting out her hands*).—Oh, Pip, don't look at
me like that ! I've never seen you look like that before, and
it hu-urts me ! I'm sorry. I oughtn't to have been here at
all, and—and—and—(*sobbing*). Oh, be good to me ! Be
good to me ! There's only you—anywhere !

Breaks down in long chair, hiding face in cushions.

CAPTAIN G. (*aside*).—She doesn't know how she flicked
me on the raw. (*Aloud, bending over chair.*) I didn't mean
to be harsh, dear—I didn't really. You can stay here as
long as you please, and do what you please. Don't cry like

that. You'll make yourself sick. (*Aside.*) What on earth
has come over her? (*Aloud.*) Darling, what's the matter
with you?

MRS. G. (*her face still hidden*).—Let me go—let me go to
my own room. Only—only say you aren't angry with me.

CAPTAIN G.—Angry with *you*, love. Of course not. I
was angry with myself. I'd lost my temper over the saddlery. Don't hide your face, Pussy. I want to kiss it.

*Bends lower, Mrs. G. slides right arm round his neck.
Several interludes and much sobbing.*

MRS. G. (*in a whisper*).—I didn't mean about the jam
when I came in to tell you ——

CAPTAIN G.—Bother the jam and the equipment! (*Interlude.*)

MRS. G. (*still more faintly*).—My finger wasn't scalded at
all. I—I wanted to speak to you about—about—something
else, and—I didn't know how.

CAPTAIN G.—Speak away, then. (*Looking into her eyes.*)
Eh! Wha—at? Minnie! Here, don't go away! You
don't mean —— ?

MRS. G. (*hysterically, backing to portière and hiding her
face in its folds*).—The—the Almost Inevitable Consequences!
(*Flits through portière as G. attempts to catch her, and bolts
herself in her own room.*)

CAPTAIN G. (*his arms full of portière*).—Oh! (*Sitting
down heavily in chair.*) I'm a brute—a pig—a bully, and a
blackguard. My poor, poor little darling! "Made to be
amused only!"

CURTAIN.

THE VALLEY OF THE SHADOW.

SCENE.—*The Gadsbys' bungalow in the Plains in June. Punkah coolies asleep in verandah where Captain Gadsby is walking up and down. Doctor's trap in porch. Junior Chaplain fluctuating generally and uneasily through the house. Time—3·40 A.M. Heat 94° in verandah.*

DOCTOR (*coming into verandah and touching G. on the shoulder*).—You had better go in and see her now.

CAPTAIN G. (*the colour of good cigar-ash*).—Eh, wha-at? Oh, yes, of course. What did you say?

DOCTOR (*syllable by syllable*).—Go—in—to—the—room—and—see—her. She wants to speak to you. (*Aside, testily.*) I shall have *him* on my hands next.

JUNIOR CHAPLAIN (*in half-lighted dining-room*).—Isn't there any ——?

DOCTOR (*savagely*).—Hsh, you little fool!

JUNIOR CHAPLAIN.—Let me do my work. Gadsby, stop a minute! (*Edges after G.*)

DOCTOR.—Wait till she sends for you at least—*at least*. Man alive, he'll kill you if you go in there! What are you bothering him for?

JUNIOR CHAPLAIN (*coming into verandah*).—I've given him a stiff brandy-peg. He wants it. You've forgotten him for the last ten hours and—forgotten yourself too.

G. enters bed-room, which is lighted by one night-lamp. Ayah on the floor pretending to be asleep.

VOICE (*from the bed*).—All down the street—*such* bonfires! Ayah, go and put them out! (*Appealingly.*) How can I sleep with an installation of the C.I.E. in my room? No—not C.I.E. Something else. *What* was it?

CAPTAIN G. (*trying to control his voice*).—Minnie, I'm here.

(*Bending over bed.*) Don't you know me, Minnie ? It's me
—it's Phil—it's your husband.

VOICE (*mechanically*).—It's me—it's Phil—it's your husband.

CAPTAIN G.—She doesn't know me! It's your own
husband, darling.

VOICE.—Your own husband, darling.

AYAH (*with an inspiration*).—*Memsahib* understanding all
I saying.

CAPTAIN G.—Make her understand me then—quick !

AYAH (*hand on Mrs. G.'s forehead*).—*Memsahib !* Captain
Sahib have sent Salaam—wanting see you.

VOICE. *Salam do.* (*Fretfully.*) I know I'm not fit to
be seen.

AYAH (*aside to G.*).—Say " *marneen* " same as at breakfash.

CAPTAIN G.—Good morning, little woman. How are we
to-day ?

VOICE.—That's Phil. Poor old Phil. (*Viciously.*) Phil,
you fool, I can't see you. Come nearer.

CAPTAIN G.—Minnie ! Minnie ! It's me—you know
me ?

VOICE (*mockingly*).—Of course I do. Who does not know
the man who was so cruel to his wife—almost the only one
he ever had ?

CAPTAIN G.—Yes, dear. Yes—of course, of course. But
won't you speak to him ? He wants to speak to you *so*
much.

VOICE.—They'd never let him in. The Doctor would
stop him even if he were in the house. He'll never come.
(*Despairingly.*) Oh Judas ! Judas ! Judas !

CAPTAIN G. (*putting out his arms*).—They have let him
in, and he always was in the house. Oh my love—don't you
know me ?

VOICE (*in a half chant*).—"And it came to pass at the
eleventh hour that this poor soul repented." It knocked at
the gates, but they were shut—tight as a plaster—a great,

burning plaster. They had pasted our marriage certificate all across the door and it was made of red-hot iron. People really ought to be more careful, you know.

CAPTAIN G.—What *am* I to do? (*Takes her in his arms.*) Minnie! speak to me—to Phil

VOICE.—What shall I say? Oh tell me what to say before it's too late! They are all going away and I can't say anything.

CAPTAIN G.—Say you know me! Only say you know me!

DOCTOR (*who has entered quietly*).—For pity's sake don't take it too much to heart, Gadsby. It's this way sometimes. They won't recognise. They say all sorts of queer things—don't you *see*?

CAPTAIN G.—All right! All right! Go away now! she'll recognise me; you're bothering her. She *must*—mustn't she, Doc.?

DOCTOR.—She will before—Have I your leave to try—

CAPTAIN G.—Anything you please so long as she'll know me. It's only a question of—hours, isn't it?

DOCTOR (*professionally*).—While there's life there's hope, y'know. But don't build on it.

CAPTAIN G.—I don't. Pull her together if it's possible. (*Aside.*) What have I done to deserve this?

DOCTOR (*bending over bed*).—Now Mrs. Gadsby. We shall be all right to-morrow—You *must* take it, or I shan't let Phil see you—It isn't nasty, is it?

VOICE.—Medicines! *Always* more medicines. Can't you leave me alone?

CAPTAIN G.—Oh leave her in peace, Doc.!

DOCTOR (*stepping back,—aside*).—May I be forgiven if I've done wrong. (*Aloud.*) In a few minutes she ought to be sensible; but I daren't tell you to look for anything. It's only ——

CAPTAIN G.—What? Go *on*, man.

DOCTOR (*in a whisper*).—Forcing the last rally.

CAPTAIN G.—Then leave us alone.

DOCTOR.—Don't mind what she says at first, if you can. They—they—they turn against those they love most sometimes in this—It's hard, but ——

CAPTAIN G.—Am I her husband or are you ? Leave us alone for whatever time we have together.

VOICE (*confidentially*).—And we were engaged *quite* suddenly, Emma. I assure you that I never thought of it for a moment ; but, O my little Me !—I don't know what I should have done if he *hadn't* proposed.

CAPTAIN G.— She thinks of that Deercourt girl before she thinks of me. (*Aloud.*) Minnie !

VOICE.—Not from the shops, Mummy dear. You can get the real leaves from Kaintu, and (*laughing weakly*) never mind about the blossoms. Dead white silk is only fit for widows, and I *won't* wear it. It's as bad as a winding-sheet. (*A long pause.*)

CAPTAIN G.—I never asked a favour yet. If there is anybody to listen to me, let her know me—even if I die too !

VOICE (*very faintly*).—Pip, Pip, dear.

CAPTAIN G.—I'm here, darling.

VOICE.—What has happened ? They've been bothering me so with medicines and things, and they wouldn't let you come and see me. I was never ill before. Am I ill now ?

CAPTAIN G.—You—you aren't quite well.

VOICE.—How funny ! Have I been ill long ?

CAPTAIN G.—Some days ; but you will be all right in a little time.

VOICE.—Do you think so, Pip ? I don't feel well and —Oh ! what *have* they done to my hair ?

CAPTAIN G.—I d-d-don't know.

VOICE—They've cut it off. What a shame !

CAPTAIN G.—It must have been to make your head cooler.

VOICE.—'Just like a boy's wig. Don't I look horrid

CAPTAIN G.—Never looked prettier in your life, dear.

(*Aside.*) How am I to ask her to say good-bye ?

VOICE.—I don't *feel* pretty. I feel very ill. My heart won't work. It's nearly dead inside me, and there's a funny feeling in my eyes. Everything seems the same distance— you and the wardrobe and the table—inside my eyes or miles away. What does it mean, Pip?

CAPTAIN G.—You're a little feverish, Sweetheart—very feverish. (*Breaking down.*) My love! my love! How can I let you go?

VOICE.—I thought so. Why didn't you tell me that at first?

CAPTAIN G.—What?

VOICE.—That I am going to—die.

CAPTAIN G.—But you aren't! You shan't!

AYAH (*stepping into verandah after a glance at the bed*).— Coolie boy—stop pulling punkah.

VOICE.—It's hard, Pip. So very, *very* hard after one year—just one year. (*Wailing.*) And I'm only twenty. Most girls aren't even married at twenty. Can't they do *anything* to help me? I don't want to die.

CAPTAIN G.—Hush, dear. You won't.

VOICE.—What's the use of talking. *Help* me! You've never failed me yet. Oh, Phil, help me to keep alive! (*Feverishly.*) I don't believe you wish me to live. You weren't a bit sorry when that horrid Baby thing died. I wish I'd killed Baby!

CAPTAIN G. (*drawing his hand across his forehead*).— It's more than a man's meant to bear—it's not right. (*Aloud.*) Minnie love, I'd die for you if it would help.

VOICE.—No more death. There's enough already. Pip, don't *you* die too.

CAPTAIN G.—I wish I dared.

VOICE.—It says:—"Till Death do us part". Nothing after that . . . and so it would be no use. It stops at the dying. Why does it stop there? Only such a very short life, too. Pip, I'm sorry we married.

CAPTAIN G.—No! Anything but that, Min!

VOICE.—Because you'll forget and I'll forget. Oh Pip,

don't forget! I always loved you, though I was cross sometimes. If I ever did anything that you didn't like say you
forgive me now.

CAPTAIN G.—You never did, darling. On my soul and
honour you never did. I haven't a thing to forgive you.

VOICE.—I sulked for a whole week about bedding out
those petunias. (*With a laugh.*) What a little wretch I was,
and how grieved you were! Forgive me that, Pip.

CAPTAIN G.—There's nothing to forgive. It was my
fault. They *were* too near the drive. For God's sake don't
talk so, Minnie! There's such a lot to say and so little time
to say it in.

VOICE.—Say that you'll always love me—until the end.

CAPTAIN G.—Until the end. (*Carried away.*) It's a lie.
It *must* be, because we've loved each other. This isn't the end.

VOICE (*relapsing into semi-delirium*). *My* Church-service
has an ivory cross on the back, and *it* says so, so it must be
true. "Till death do us part." But that's a lie. (*With
a parody of G.'s manner.*) A damned lie! (*Recklessly.*)
Yes, I can swear as well as Trooper Pip. I can't make
my head think, though. That's because they cut off my
hair. How *can* one think with one's head all fuzzy?
(*Pleadingly.*) Hold me, Pip! Keep me with you always
and always. (*Relapsing.*) But if you marry the Thorniss
girl when I'm dead, I'll come back and howl under our bed-
room window all night. Oh bother! You'll think I'm
jackals. Pip, what time is it?

CAPTAIN G.—A little before the dawn, dear.

VOICE.—I wonder where I shall be this time to-morrow?

CAPTAIN G.—Would you like to see the Padre?

VOICE.—Why should I? He'd tell me that I am going
to Heaven; and that wouldn't be true, because you are here.
Do you recollect when he upset the cream-ice all over his
trousers at the Gassers' tennis?

CAPTAIN G.—Yes, dear.

VOICE.—I often wondered whether he got another pair

of trousers; but then his are so shiny all over, that you really couldn't tell unless you were told. Let's call him in and ask.

CAPTAIN G. (*gravely*).—No. I don't think he'd like that. 'Your head comfy, Sweetheart?

VOICE (*faintly, with a sigh of contentment*).—Yeth Gracious Pip, when *did* you shave last? Your chin's worse than the barrel of a musical-box. No, don't lift it up. like it. (*A pause.*) You said you've never cried at all. You're crying all over my cheek.

CAPTAIN G.—I—I—I can't help it, dear.

VOICE.—How funny! I couldn't cry now to save my life. (*G. shivers.*) *I* want to sing.

CAPTAIN G.—Won't it tire you? 'Better not, perhaps.

VOICE.—Why? I *won't* be ordered about! (*Begins in a hoarse quaver*) :—

> Minnie bakes oaten cake, Minnie brews ale,
> All because her Johnnie's coming home from the sea (That's parade, Pip),
> And she grows red as rose who was so pale :
> And "are you sure the church-clock goes?" says she.

(*Pettishly.*) I knew I couldn't take the last note. How do the bass chords run? (*Puts out her hands and begins playing piano on the sheet.*)

CAPTAIN G. (*catching up hands*). Ah! Don't do that, Pussy, if you love me.

VOICE.—Love you? Of course I do. Who else should it be? (*A pause.*)

VOICE (*very clearly*).—Pip, I'm going now. Something's choking me cruelly. (*Indistinctly.*) Into the dark— without you, my heart. But it's a lie, dear—we mustn't believe it. For ever and ever, living or dead. Don't let me go, my husband—hold me tight. They can't—whatever happens. (*A cough.*) Pip—*my* Pip! Not for always —and—so—soon! (*Voice ceases.*)

Pause of ten minutes. G. buries his face in the side of the bed, while Ayah bends over bed from opposite side and feels Mrs. G.'s breast and forehead.

CAPTAIN G. (*rising*).—Ayah, tell the Doctor.

AYAH (*still by bedside, with a shriek*).—Ai! Ai! Breaking! My *Memsahib!* Not getting—not have got—broken fever now —sweat have come! *(Fiercely to G.) You* go tell Doctor! *Oh,* my *Memsahib!*

DOCTOR (*entering hastily*).—Come away, Gadsby. *(Bends over bed.)* Eh? The dev—— What inspired you to stop the punkah? Get out, man—go away—wait outside! *Go!* Here Ayah? *(Over his shoulder to G.)* Mind, I promise nothing.

The dawn breaks as G. stumbles into the garden.

CAPTAIN MAFFLIN (*reining up at the gate, on his way to parade, and very soberly*).—Old man, how goes?

CAPTAIN G. (*dazed*).—I don't quite know. Stay a bit. Have a drink or something. Don't run away. You're just getting amusing. Ha! ha!

CAPTAIN M. (*aside*).—What *am* I let in for? Gaddy has aged ten years in the night.

CAPTAIN G. (*slowly, fingering charger's headstall*).—Your curb's too loose.

CAPTAIN M.—So it is. Put it straight, will you? *(Aside.)* I shall be late for parade. Poor Gaddy.

Captain G. links and unlinks curb-chain aimlessly, and finally stands staring towards the verandah. The day brightens.

DOCTOR (*knocked out of professional gravity, tramping across flower-beds and shaking G.'s hands*).—It's—it's—it's!— Gadsby, there's a fair chance—a *dashed* fair chance! The flicker y'know. The sweat y'know! I *saw* how it would be. The punkah, y'know. Deuced clever woman that Ayah of yours. Just at the right time. A *dashed* good chance! No —you don't go in. We'll pull her through yet. I promise on my reputation—under Providence. Send a man with this note to Bingle. Two heads better than one. 'Specially the Ayah! *We'll* pull her round. *(Retreats hastily to house.)*

CAPTAIN G. (*his head on neck of M.'s charger*).—Jack! I

bub—bub—believe I'm going to make a bub—bub—blasted exhibitiod of byself.

CAPTAIN M. (*sniffing openly and feeling in his left cuff*).— I b—b—believe I'b doing it already. Old bad, what *cad* I say? I'b as pleased as—Cod *dab* you, Gaddy! You're one big idiot and I'b adother. (*Pulling himself together.*) Sit tight! Here comes the Devil Dodger.

JUNIOR CHAPLAIN (*who is not in the Doctor's confidence*).— We—we are only men in these things, Gadsby. I know that I can say nothing now to help——

CAPTAIN M. (*jealously*).—Then don't say it! Leave him alone. It's not bad enough to croak over. Here, Gaddy, take the note to Bingle and ride hell-for-leather. It'll do you good. I can't go.

JUNIOR CHAPLAIN.—Do him good! (*Smiling.*) Give it me and I'll drive. Let him lie down. Your horse is blocking my cart — sir!

CAPTAIN M. (*slowly, without reining back*).—I beg your pardon—I'll apologise. On paper if you like.

JUNIOR CHAPLAIN (*flicking M.'s charger*).—That'll do, thanks. Turn in, Gadsby, and I'll bring Bingle back—ahem —"hell-for-leather".

CAPTAIN M. (*solus*).—It would ha' served me right if he had cut me across the face. He can drive too. I shouldn't care to go that pace in a bamboo-cart. What a faith he must have in his Maker—of harness! Come *hup*, you brute! (*Gallops off to parade, blowing his nose, as the sun rises.*)

INTERVAL OF FIVE WEEKS.

MRS. G. (*very white and pinched, in morning wrapper at breakfast table*).—How big and strange the room looks, and, oh, how glad I am to see it again! What dust, though! I must talk to the servants. Sugar, Pip? I've almost forgotten. (*Seriously.*) Wasn't I very ill?

CAPTAIN G.—Iller than I liked. (*Tenderly.*) Oh, you bad little Pussy, what a start you gave me

6

Mrs. G.—I'll never do it again.

Captain G.—You'd better not. And now get those poor pale cheeks pink again, or I shall be angry. Don't try to lift the urn. You'll upset it. Wait. (*Comes round to head of table and lifts urn.*)

Mrs. G. (*quickly*).—Butler, go and fetch the kettle. (*Drawing down G.'s face to her own.*) Pip, dear, *I* remember.

Captain G.—What?

Mrs. G.—That last terrible night.

Captain G.—Then, just you forget all about it.

Mrs. G. (*softly, her eyes filling*).—Never. It has brought us *very* close together, my husband. There! (*Interlude.*) I'm going to give Junda a new cloth.

Captain G.—I gave her fifty rupees.

Mrs. G.—So she told me. It was a 'normous reward. Was I worth it? (*Several interludes.*) Don't! Here's the servant. Two lumps or one, sir?

CURTAIN.

THE SWELLING OF JORDAN.

"If thou hast run with the footmen and they have wearied thee, then how
canst thou contend with horses? And if in the land of peace wherein
thou trustedst they have wearied thee, how wilt thou do in the swelling
of Jordan?"

SCENE.—*The Gadsby's bungalow in the Plains, on a January morning. Mrs. G. arguing with bearer in back verandah. Captain Mafflin rides up.*

CAPTAIN M.—'Mornin', Mrs. Gadsby. How's the Infant Phenomenon and the Proud Proprietor?

MRS. G.—You'll find them in the front verandah; go through the house. I'm Martha just now.

CAPTAIN M.—'Cumbered about with cares of housekeeping? I fly.

Passes into front verandah, where Gadsby is watching Gadsby junior, ætat. ten months, crawling about the matting.

CAPTAIN M.—What's the trouble, Gaddy—spoiling an honest man's Europe morning this way? (*Seeing G., junior.*) By Jove, that yearling's comin' on amazingly! Any amount of bone below the knee there.

CAPTAIN G.—Yes, he's a healthy little scoundrel. Don't you think his hair's growing?

M.—Let's have a look. Hi! Hst! Come here, General Luck, and we'll report on you.

MRS. G. (*within*).—What absurd name will you give him next? Why do you call him that?

M.—Isn't he our Inspector-General of Cavalry? Doesn't he come down in his seventeen-two perambulator every morning the Pink Hussars parade? Don't wriggle, Brigadier. Give us your private opinion on the way the third squadron went past. 'Trifle ragged, weren't they?

G.—A bigger set of tailors than the new draft I don't wish to see. They've given me more than my fair share—knocking the squadron out of shape. It's sickening.

M.—When you're in command, you'll do better, young 'un. Can't you walk yet? Grip my finger and try. (*To G.*) 'Twon't hurt his hocks, will it?

G.—Oh, no. Don't let him flop, though, or he'll lick all the blacking off your boots.

Mrs. G. (*within*).—Who's destroying my son's character?

M.—And my Godson's? I'm ashamed of you, Gaddy. Punch your father in the eye, Jack! Don't you stand it! Hit him again!

G. (*sotto voce*).—Put The *Butcha* down and come to the end of the verandah. I'd rather the Wife didn't hear—just now.

M.—You look awf'ly serious. Anything wrong?

G.—'Depends on your view entirely. I say, Jack, you won't think more hardly of me than you can help, will you? Come further this way. The fact of the matter is, that I've made up my mind—at least I'm thinking seriously of —cutting the Service.

M.—Hwhatt??

G.—Don't shout. I'm going to send in my papers.

M.—You! Are you mad?

G.—No—only married.

M.—Look here! What's the meaning of it all? You never intend to leave *us*. You *can't*. Isn't the best squadron of the best regiment of the best cavalry in all the world good enough for you?

G. (*jerking his head over his shoulder*).—She doesn't seem to thrive in this God-forsaken country, and there's The *Butcha* to be considered, and all that, you know.

M.—Does she say that she doesn't like India?

Mrs. G.—That's the worst of it. She won't, for fear of leaving me.

M.—What are the Hills made for?

G.—Not for *my* wife, at any rate.

M.—You know too much, Gaddy, and—I don't like you any the better for it!

G.—Never mind that. She wants England, and The

Butcha would be all the better for it. I'm going to chuck. You don't understand.

M. (*hotly*).—I understand *this*. One hundred and thirty-seven new horses to be licked into shape somehow before Luck comes round again ; a hairy-heeled draft who'll give more trouble than the horses ; a camp next cold weather for a certainty ; ourselves the first on the roster ; the Russian shindy ready to come to a head at five minutes' notice, and you, the best of us all, backing out of it all ! Think a little, Gaddy. You *won't* do it.

G.—Hang it, a man has some duties towards his family, I suppose.

M.—I remember a man, though, who told me, the night after Amdheran, when we were picketted under Jagai, and he'd left his sword—by the way, did you ever pay Ranken for that sword ?—in an Utmanzai's head—that man told me that he'd stick by me and the Pinks as long as he lived. I don't blame him for not sticking by me—I'm not much of a man—but I *do* blame him for not sticking by the Pink Hussars.

G. (*uneasily*).—We were little more than boys then. Can't you see, Jack, how things stand ? 'Tisn't as if we were serving for our bread. We've all of us, more or less, got the filthy lucre. I'm luckier than some, perhaps. There's no *call* for me to serve on.

M.—None in the world for you or for us, except the Regimental. If you don't choose to answer to *that*, of course ——

G.—Don't be too hard on a man. You know that a lot of us only take up the thing for a few years, and then go back to Town and catch on with the rest.

M.—Not lots, and they aren't some of *Us*.

G.—And then there are one's affairs at Home to be considered—my place and the rents, and all that. I don't suppose my father can last much longer, and that means the title, and so on.

M.—'Fraid you won't be entered in the Stud Book correctly unless you go Home? Take six months, then, and come out in October. If I could slay off a brother or two, I s'pose I should be a Marquis of sorts. Any fool can be that; but it needs *men*, Gaddy—men like you—to lead flanking squadrons properly. Don't you delude yourself into the belief that you're going Home to take your place, and prance about among pink-nosed dowagers. You aren't built that way. I know better.

G.—A man has a right to live his life as happily as he can. *You* aren't married.

M.—No—praise be to Providence and the one or two women who have had the good sense to *jawab* me.

G.—Then you don't know what it is to go into your own room and see your wife's head on the pillow, and when everything else is safe, and the house *bunded* up for the night, to wonder whether the roof-beams won't give and kill her.

M. (*aside*).—Revelations first and second! (*Aloud.*) So-o! I knew a man who got squiffy at our Mess once and confided to me that he never helped his wife on to her horse without praying that she'd break her neck before she came back. All husbands aren't alike, you see.

G.—What on earth has that to do with my case? The man must ha' been mad, or his wife as bad as they make 'em.

M. (*aside*).—No fault of yours if either weren't all you say. You've forgotten the time when you were insane about the Herriott woman. You always were a good hand at forgetting. (*Aloud.*) Not more mad than men who go to the other extreme. Be reasonable, Gaddy. Your roof-beams are sound enough.

G.—That was only a way of speaking. I've been uneasy and worried about the wife ever since that awful business three years ago when—I nearly lost her. Can you wonder?

M.—Oh, a shell never falls twice in the same place.

You've paid your toll to misfortune—why should your wife be picked out more than anybody else's?

G.—I can *talk* just as reasonably as you can, but you don't understand—you don't understand. And then there's The *Butcha*. Deuce knows where the ayah takes him to sit in the evening! He has a bit of a cough. Haven't you noticed it?

M.—Bosh! The Brigadier's jumping out of his skin with pure condition. He's got a muzzle like a rose-leaf and the chest of a two-year old. What's demoralised you?

G.—Funk. That's the long and the short of it. Funk!

M.—But what *is* there to funk?

G.—Everything. It's ghastly.

M.—Ah! I see. " You don't want to fight,
And by Jingo when we do,
You've got the kid, you've got the wife,
You've got the money, too."

That's about the case, eh?

G.—I suppose that's it. But it's not for myself. It's because of *them*. At least, I think it is.

M.—Are you sure? Looking at the matter in a cold-blooded light, the wife is provided for even if you were wiped out to-night. She has an ancestral home to go to, money, and The Brigadier to carry on the illustrious name.

G.—Then it is for myself or because they are part of me. You don't see it. My life's so good, so pleasant, as it is, that I want to make it quite safe. Can't you understand?

M.—Perfectly. " Shelter-pit for the Orf'cer's charger," as they say in the Line.

G.—And I have everything to my hand to make it so. I'm sick of the strain and the worry for their sakes out here; and there isn't a single real difficulty to prevent my dropping it altogether. It'll only cost me—Jack, I hope you'll never know the shame that I've been going through for the past six months.

M.—Hold on there! I don't wish to be told. Every man has his moods and tenses sometimes.

G. (*laughing bitterly*).—Has he? What do you call craning over to see where your brute's near-fore lands?

M.—In my case it means that I have been on the Considerable Bend, and have come to parade with a Head and a Hand. It passes in three strides.

G. (*lowering voice*).—It *never* passes with me, Jack. I'm always thinking about it. Phil Gadsby funking a fall on parade! Sweet picture, isn't it? Draw it for me.

M. (*gravely*).—Heaven forbid! A man like you can't be as bad as that. A fall is no nice thing, but one never gives it a thought.

G.—Doesn't one? Wait till you've got a wife and a youngster of your own, and then you'll know how the roar of the squadron behind you turns you cold all up the back.

M. (*aside*).—And this man led at Amdheran after Bagal-Deasin went under, and we were all mixed up together, and he came out of the show dripping like a butcher! (*Aloud.*) Skittles! The men can always open out, and you can always pick your way more or less. *We* haven't the dust to bother us, as the men have, and who ever heard of a horse stepping on a man?

G.—Never—as long as he can see. But did they open out for poor Errington?

M.—Oh, this is childish!

G.—I know it is, and worse than that. I don't care. You've ridden *Van Loo*. Is he the sort of animal to pick his way—'specially when we're coming up in column of troop with any pace on?

M.—Once in a Blue Moon do we gallop in column of troop, and then only to save time. Aren't three lengths enough for you?

G.—Yes—quite enough. They just allow for the full development of the smash. I'm talking like a cur, I know; but I tell you that, for the past three months, I've felt every

hoof of the squadron in the small of my back every time that
I've led.

M.—But, Gaddy, this is awful !

G.—Isn't it lovely ? Isn't it royal ? A Captain of the
Pink Hussars watering up his charger before parade like the
blasted boozing Colonel of a Black Regiment ?

M.—You never did !

G.—Once only. He squelched like a *mussuck*, and the
Troop-Sergeant-Major cocked his eye at me. You know old
Hafty's eye. I was afraid to do it again.

M.—I should think so. That was the best way to
rupture old *Van Loo's* tummy, and make him crumple you
up. You *knew* that.

G.—I didn't care. It took the edge off him.

M.—Took the edge off him ! Gaddy, you—you—you
mustn't, you know ! Think of the men.

G.—That's another thing I am afraid of. D'you s'pose
they know.

M.—Let's hope not; but they're deadly quick to spot
skrim—little things of that kind. See here, old man, send
the wife home for the hot weather and come to Kashmir with
me. We'll start a boat on the Dal or cross the Rhotang—
ibex or idleness—which you please. Only *come !* You're a
bit off your oats, and you're talking nonsense. Look at the
Colonel—swag-bellied rascal that he is. He has a wife and
no end of a bow-window of his own. Can any one of us ride
round him—chalkstones and all ? *I* can't, and I think I can
shove a crock along a bit.

G.—Some men are different. I haven't the nerve. Lord
help me, I haven't the nerve ! I've taken up a hole and a
half to get my knees well under the wallets. I can't help
it. I'm so afraid of anything happening to me. On my soul
I ought to be broke in front of the squadron for cowardice.

M.—Ugly word, that. I should never have the courage
to own up.

G.—I meant to lie about my reasons when I began, but

—I've got out of the habit of lying to you, old man. Jack, you won't?—But I know you won't.

M.—Of course not. (*Half aloud.*) The Pinks are paying dearly for their Pride.

G.—Eh! Wha-at?

M.—Don't you know? We've called Mrs. Gadsby the Pride of the Pink Hussars ever since she came to us.

G.—'Tisn't *her* fault. Don't think that. It's all mine.

M.—What does she say?

G.—I haven't exactly put it before her. She's the best little woman in the world, Jack, and all that,—but she wouldn't counsel a man to stick to his calling if it came between him and her. At least, I think ——

M.—Never mind. Don't tell her what you told me. Go on the Peerage and Landed-Gentry tack.

G.—She'd see through it. She's five times cleverer than I am.

M. (*aside*).—Then she'll accept the sacrifice, and think a little bit worse of him for the rest of her days.

G. (*absently*).—I say, do you despise me?

M.—'Queer way of putting it. Have you ever been asked that question? Think a minute. What answer used you to give?

G.—So bad as *that?* I'm not entitled to expect anything more; but it's a bit hard when one's best friend turns round and ——

M.—So *I* have found. But you will have consolations —Bailiffs and Drains and Liquid Manure and the Primrose League, and, perhaps, if you're lucky, the Colonelcy of a Yeomanry Cav-al-ry Regiment—all uniform and no riding, I believe. How old are you?

G.—Thirty-three. I know it's ——

M.—At forty you'll be a fool of a J. P. landlord. At fifty you'll own a bath-chair, and The Brigadier, if he takes after you, will be fluttering the dovecots of—what's the particular dunghill you're going to? Also, Mrs. Gadsby will be fat.

G. (*limply*).—This is rather more than a joke.

M.—D'you think so? Isn't cutting the Service a joke? It generally takes a man fifty years to arrive at it. You're quite right, though. It is more than a joke. You've managed it in thirty-three.

G.—Don't make me feel worse than I do. Will it satisfy you if I own that I am a shirker, a skrimshanker and a coward?

M.—It will *not*, because I'm the only man in the world who can talk to you like this without being knocked down. You mustn't take all that I've said to heart in this way. I only spoke—a lot of it at least—out of pure selfishness, be-cause, because—Oh, damn it all, old man—I don't know what I shall do without you. Of course, you've got the money and the place and all that—and there are two very good reasons why you should take care of yourself.

G.—'Doesn't make it any the sweeter. I'm backing out —I know I am. I always had a soft drop in me somewhere —and I daren't risk any danger to *them*.

M.—Why in the world should you? You're bound to think of your family—bound to think. Er-hmm. If I wasn't a younger son I'd go too—be shot if I wouldn't!

G.—Thank you, Jack. It's a kind lie, but it's the blackest you've told for some time. I know what I'm doing, and I'm going into it with my eyes open. Old man, I *can't* help it. What would you do if you were in my place?

M. (*aside*).—'Couldn't conceive any woman getting per-manently between me and the Regiment. (*Aloud.*) 'Can't say. 'Very likely I should do no better. I'm sorry for you —awf'ly sorry—but " if them's your sentiments," I believe, I really do, that you are acting wisely.

G.—Do you? I hope you do. (*In a whisper.*) Jack, be very sure of yourself before you marry. I'm an ungrateful ruffian to say this, but marriage—even as good a marriage as mine has been—hamper's a man's work, it cripples his sword-arm, and Oh! it plays Hell with his notions of duty! Sometimes—good and sweet as she is—sometimes I could wish that I had kept my freedom. No, I don't mean that exactly.

MRS. G. (*coming down verandah*).—What are you wagging your head over, Pip?

M. (*turning quickly*).—Me, as usual. The old sermon. Your husband is recommending me to get married. 'Never saw such a one-idead man!

MRS. G.—Well, why don't you? I daresay you would make some woman very happy.

G.—There's the Law and the Prophets, Jack. Never mind the Regiment. Make a woman happy. (*Aside.*) O Lord!

M.—We'll see. I must be off to make a Troop Cook desperately unhappy. I won't have the wily Hussar fed on G. B. T. shin-bones. (*Hastily.*) Surely black ants can't be good for The Brigadier. He's picking 'em off the floor and eating 'em. Here, Senor Commandante Don Grubbynose, come and talk to me. (*Lifts G., junior, in his arms.*) 'Want my watch? You won't be able to put it into your mouth, but you can try. (*G., junior, drops watch, breaking dial and hands.*)

MRS. G.—Oh Captain Mafflin, I *am* so sorry! Jack, you bad, bad little villain. Ahhh!

M.—It's not the least consequence, I assure you. He'd treat the world in the same way if he could get it into his hands. Everything's made to be played with and broken, isn't it, young 'un? (*Tenderly.*) "Oh Diamond, Diamond, thou little knowest the mischief that thou hast done."

·   ·   ·   ·   ·   ·   ·   ·   ·   ·

MRS. G.—Mafflin didn't at all like his watch being broken, though he was too polite to say so. It was entirely his fault for giving it to the child. Dem little puds are werry, werry feeble, aren't dey, my Jack-in-the-box? (*To G.*) What did he want to see you for?

G.—Regimental shop o' sorts.

MRS. G.—The Regiment! *Always* the Regiment. On my word I sometimes feel jealous of Mafflin.

G. (*wearily*).—Poor old Jack! I don't think you need. Isn't it time for The *Butcha* to have his nap? Bring a chair out here, dear. I've got something to talk over with you.

AND THIS IS THE END OF THE STORY OF THE GADSBYS.

L'ENVOI.

WHAT is the moral? Who rides may read.
　　When the night is thick and the tracks are blind,
A friend at a pinch is a friend indeed;
　　But a fool to wait for the laggard behind:
Down to Gehenna, or up to the Throne,
He travels the fastest who travels alone.

White hands cling to the tightened rein,
　　Slipping the spur from the booted heel,
Tenderest voices cry, "Turn again,"
　　Red lips tarnish the scabbarded steel,
High hopes faint on a warm hearth-stone—
He travels the fastest who travels alone.

One may fall, but he falls by himself—
　　Falls by himself, with himself to blame;
One may attain, and to him is the pelf,
　　Loot of the city in Gold or Fame:
Plunder of earth shall be all his own
Who travels the fastest, and travels alone.

Wherefore the more ye be holpen and stayed—
　　Stayed by a friend in the hour of toil,
Sing the heretical song I have made—
　　His be the labour, and yours be the spoil.
Win by his aid, and the aid disown—
He travels the fastest who travels alone.

Printed at the "Pioneer Press", Allahabad.

PUBLICATIONS OF
THE R. S. SURTEES SOCIETY

R. S. SURTEES

Mr. Sponge's Sporting Tour. Facsimile of 1853 edition. 13 full-page coloured plates and 90 engravings by **John Leech**. Introduction by **Auberon Waugh**.

Mr. Facey Romford's Hounds. 24 coloured plates by **Leech** and **'Phiz'**. 50 engravings by **W. T. Maud**. Introduction by **Enoch Powell**.

"Ask Mamma". Facsimile of 1858 edition, 13 coloured plates and 70 engravings by **Leech**. Introduction by **Rebecca West**.

Handley Cross; or **Mr. Jorrocks' Hunt.** Facsimile of 1854 edition. 17 coloured plates and 100 engravings by **Leech**. Introduction by **Raymond Carr**.

Jorrocks' Jaunts and Jollities. Facsimile of 1874 edition. 31 coloured plates by **Henry Alken, 'Phiz'** and **W. Heath**. Introduction by **Michael Wharton** ('Peter Simple').

Hillingdon Hall or **The Cockney Squire** (Mr. Jorrocks). Facsimile of 1888 edition. 12 coloured plates by **Wildrake, W. Heath** and **Jellicoe**. Introduction by **Robert Blake**.

Plain or Ringlets? Facsimile of 1860 edition. 13 coloured plates and 45 engravings by **Leech**. Introduction by **Molly Keane**.

Price **£14.95** in each case, packing and postage included.

Separate sets of coloured plates **£5** each (including p. & p.)

The Horseman's Manual: being a treatise on Soundness, of the Law of Warranty and generally on the Laws relating to Horses. Surtees's first book, published in 1831. Hugh Davidson has published a numbered facsimile edition of 600 copies, of which 38 remain.

Price **£10.50,** packing and postage included.

John Leech
and the Victorian Scene

Simon Houfe's magnificent book on Leech (published by the Antique Collectors' Club) is offered to all subscribers for books of the R. S. Surtees Society, whether under this or previous offers, at the price of **£19.50** (including p. & p.), compared with the normal retail price of £22.50.

It contains 130 illustrations, many in colour.

SOME EXPERIENCES *AND* FURTHER EXPERIENCES OF AN IRISH R.M. *AND* IN MR. KNOX'S COUNTRY

by E. OE. Somerville and Martin Ross.

Some Experiences, Further Experiences and *In Mr. Knox's Country* contain thirty-five episodes in which Major Sinclair Yeates recounts, with sober dignity, humour and tolerance, his social and professional discomfitures as a Resident Magistrate in South-West Ireland at the turn of the century. The rhetoric and deceit of the natives provide the wit and drama. Circumstances make Major Yeates a connoisseur of whole-hearted insincerity.

The R. S. Surtees Society's editions of *Some Experiences, Further Experiences* and *In Mr. Knox's Country* are as nearly as practicable facsimiles of the first editions, of 1899, 1908 and 1915 respectively. They include the black and white illustrations by **Miss Somerville** from the first editions (30 in *Some Experiences,* 35 in *Further Experiences* and 8 in *Mr. Knox*). Introduction by **Molly Keane**.

Price **£7.95** in each case, packing and postage included.

IRISH R.M. SET OF THREE

The price of a set of *In Mr. Knox's Country, Some Experiences* and *Further Experiences of an Irish R.M.* is **£21.00,** including packing and postage.

CAPTAIN GRONOW'S REMINISCENCES AND RECOLLECTIONS *AND* LAST RECOLLECTIONS

Gronow served in the Peninsula War, fought at Quartre Bras and Waterloo and was with the allied armies in Paris when the Bourbons were restored. Thereafter, in London and Paris, he lived the life of a dandy "committing the greatest follies without in the slightest disturbing the points of his shirt collar." As a ranconteur he is superb, with vivid accounts of Waterloo, the coup d'etat of 1851, of balls and battles, of duellists, gamblers, dukes and opera singers.

The Society's editions are facsimiles of the Joseph Grego editions of 1889 and include all his 25 coloured plates from original and contemporary sources – "and a very handsome set they make" – Paul Johnson in The Spectator.

Prices **£14.95** for *Reminiscences and Recollections,* **£13.95** for *Last Recollections.*

GOOD INTENTIONS in WAPPING

SHIP'S COMPANY   by W. W. JACOBS

What was Wapping like before Rupert Murdoch, before the G.L.C., before the Port of London Authority, before the Germans bombed it flat, indeed before the First War and before the Trades Disputes Act, 1906 had had much effect—in fact only a decade after the Diamond Jubilee?

W. W. Jacobs (1863–1943) was born and brought up in Wapping where his father was a wharfinger. According to Michael Sadleir, in the D.N.B., he recalled his childhood days, when "with his brothers and sisters he ran wild in Wapping, as happy interludes in a life of nagging discomfort."

Like Conrad, Kipling and E. Nesbit he was a contributor to the Strand Magazine in its great days. Like Surtees, Jacobs was well served by his illustrators. He was popular with high, middle and low brows from about 1895 to 1930, by which latter date P. G. Wodehouse had overtaken him.

Jacobs' best short stories were about Wapping and the best of these were told by the night-watchman who, sitting on his wharf, recounted the adventures of his friends Sam Small, Peter Russet, Ginger Dick and others.

W. W. Jacobs' SHIP'S COMPANY is a set of 12 short stories, first published in 1908. The title is uninformative and perhaps a little misleading since the action all takes place on land—near, but not on, salt water. Some of the characters, it is true, arrive and depart by sea.

The best of all the stories in SHIP'S COMPANY is *Good Intentions,* in which the night-watchman is both the hero and the narrator. The plot is complicated, but entirely clear and credible—in fact, better and faster than the plots of most French farces. *Good Intentions in Wapping* might have been a better title for the set than SHIP'S COMPANY.

The R. S. Surtees Society's edition is a facsimile of the first (1908) edition and includes the 23 black and white illustrations by **Will Owen** in the first edition. Will Owen (1869–1957) was a Punch artist, a close friend of W. W. Jacobs and, like Leech, 'Phiz' and Edith Somerville, was completely familiar with the subjects he was drawing. It was he who drew the famous Bisto Kids advertisement.